MAIN STREET

The Revolt of Carol Kennicott

Martin Bucco

TWAYNE PUBLISHERS • NEW YORK
Maxwell Macmillan Canada • Toronto
Maxwell Macmillan International • New York Oxford Singapore Sydney

Twayne's Masterwork Studies No. 124

Twayne Publishers
Macmillan Publishing Company
866 Third Avenue
New York, New York 10022

Maxwell Macmillan Canada, Inc.
1200 Eglinton Avenue East
Suite 200
Don Mills, Ontario M3C 3N1

Library of Congress Cataloging-in-Publication Data
Bucco, Martin.
Main Street : the revolt of Carol Kennicott / Martin Bucco.
p. cm.—(Twayne's masterwork studies ; no. 124)
Includes bibliographical references [illegible]
ISBN 0-8057-8373-3 (hard).—ISBN 0-8057-8377-6 (soft)
1. Lewis, Sinclair, 1885–1951. Main Street I. Title. II. Series.
PS3523.E94M19 1993
813'.52—dc20 93-7659
CIP

The paper used in this publication meets the minimum requirements of American National Standard for Information Sciences—Permanence of Paper for Printed Library Materials, ANSI Z39.48-1984. ∞ ™

10 9 8 7 6 5 4 3 2 1 (alk. paper)
10 9 8 7 6 5 4 3 2 1 (pbk.: alk. paper)

Printed in the United States of America.

MAIN STREET

The Revolt of Carol Kennicott

TWAYNE'S MASTERWORK STUDIES

Robert Lecker, General Editor

For Greg, Lisa, and Sara

Contents

Note on the References and Acknowledgments ix
Chronology: Sinclair Lewis's Life and Works xi

LITERARY AND HISTORICAL CONTEXT
1. Historical Background 3
2. The Importance of *Main Street* 9
3. Critical Reception 13

A READING
4. Prairie Princess 25
5. Carol D'Arc 47
6. Lady Bountiful 64
7. *Mater Dolorosa* 76
8. Village Intellectual 85
9. American Bovary 98
10. Passionate Pilgrim 114

Notes 129
Selected Bibliography 131
Index 135

Note on the References and Acknowledgments

All references to *Main Street* in this volume are keyed to the New American Library edition (Signet Classic) published in 1961 and appear in parentheses in the text.

My thanks go to Colorado State University for a semester sabbatical abroad . . . to professors Warren French, Philip Melling, and Jon Roper of the University of Wales at Swansea for asylum . . . to Emily Taylor for referencing . . . to India Koopman for editing . . . and to my wife, Edith Erickson Bucco, for much more than typing the manuscript.

Sinclair Lewis, 1920
Photo: St. Paul Pioneer Press. From the collection of the Minnesota Historical Society.

Chronology: Sinclair Lewis's Life and Works

1885	In Minnesota wheat-town of Sauk Centre, Harry Sinclair Lewis, youngest of three sons, born to Emma Kermott Lewis and Edwin J. Lewis on 7 February.
1890–1902	Attends Sauk Centre public schools. Performs odd jobs for *Sauk Centre Herald* and *Sauk Centre Avalanche.*
1891–1892	Mother dies. Father marries Isabel Warner.
1902–1903	Attends Oberlin Academy, Ohio, for six months to prepare for Yale College. Matriculates at Yale. Contributes to *Yale Literary Magazine* and *Yale Courant.*
1904	Summer cattleboat trip to England.
1905	Summer in Sauk Centre. Plans a novel, *The Village Virus.*
1906	Second summer cattleboat trip to England. Works as janitor at Upton Sinclair's experiment in communal living at Helicon Hall, Englewood, New Jersey.
1907–1908	Translates German and French stories for *Transatlantic Tales* in New York. Seeks work and literary material in Panama. Returns to Yale. Works part-time for *New Haven Journal and Courier.* Graduates in June.
1908–1909	Wanders the United States as journalist and free-lance writer: Iowa, New York, California, District of Columbia, and back to New York.
1910–1915	Employed by various New York publishers as manuscript reader, editor, advertising manager, book reviewer.
1912	Boys' book, *Hike and the Aeroplane,* published under pseudonym Tom Graham.
1914	First novel, *Our Mr. Wrenn,* published. Marries Grace Livingston Hegger in New York.
1915	Second novel, *The Trail of the Hawk,* published. Resigns from George H. Doran Company to write full-time.

1916	Summer travel by automobile from Sauk Centre to Seattle. Sells stories and serials to popular magazines.
1917	Third and fourth novels, *The Job* and *The Innocents,* published. Birth of first son, Wells.
1918	Moves to St. Paul and then to Minneapolis.
1919	Fifth novel, *Free Air*, published. First play, *Hobohemia,* produced in Greenwich Village. Moves to Washington, D.C.
1920	Sixth novel, *Main Street,* published in October.
1921–1922	Lectures and travels in Europe.
1922	Seventh novel, *Babbitt,* published. Lives in Hartford, Connecticut.
1923–1925	Caribbean cruise with Paul de Kruif to gather material for *Arrowsmith.* European travel. Summer of 1924 with brother Claude in Canada.
1925	Eighth novel, *Arrowsmith,* published.
1926	Ninth novel, *Mantrap,* published. Gathers material in Kansas for *Elmer Gantry*. Declines Pulitzer Prize for *Arrowsmith.* Lives in Pequot, Minnesota. Father dies. Lewis returns to Washington, D.C.
1927	Separation from Grace Hegger Lewis. Tenth novel, *Elmer Gantry,* published.
1928	Divorces first wife. Marries journalist Dorothy Thompson in London. Eleventh novel, *The Man Who Knew Coolidge,* published.
1928–1937	Buys Twin Farms in Bernard, Vermont. Summers there; winters in New York.
1929	Twelfth novel, *Dodsworth,* published. Researches never-completed labor novel.
1930	Birth of second son, Michael. First American to win Nobel Prize in Literature; accepts award in Stockholm.
1933	Thirteenth novel, *Ann Vickers,* published.
1934	Fourteenth novel, *Work of Art,* published. Assists Sidney Howard in dramatization of *Dodsworth.* Writes second play, *Jayhawkers,* with Lloyd Lewis for New York production.
1935	*Selected Short Stories* and fifteenth novel, *It Can't Happen Here,* published. Elected to National Institute of Arts and Letters.

1936	European travel. Receives honorary degree from Yale. Federal Theater Project produces *It Can't Happen Here,* dramatized by Lewis and John C. Moffitt, in 15 American cities.
1937–1951	Travels to Bermuda. Separation from Dorothy Thompson. Lecturer, book columnist for *Newsweek,* actor, playwright, producer, director. Winters in Manhattan hotels, summers near summer theaters. Trips to Midwest, Hollywood, Florida, and other places at home and abroad.
1938	Sixteenth novel, *Prodigal Parents,* published. On tour until 1939 with his play, *Angela Is Twenty-Two.*
1940	Seventeenth novel, *Bethel Merriday,* published. Lives in Madison and teaches writing class at University of Wisconsin.
1942	Divorces second wife. Lives in Minneapolis and lectures at the University of Minneapolis.
1943	Eighteenth novel, *Gideon Planish,* published.
1944	First son, lieutenant in World War II, killed in action. Lewis buys home in Duluth.
1945	Nineteenth novel, *Cass Timberlane,* published. Reviews books for *Esquire.*
1946–1949	Moves to and later buys Thorvale Farm in Williamstown, Massachusetts.
1947	Twentieth novel, *Kingsblood Royal,* published. Historical research in Minnesota.
1948–1951	Health fails. Spends much time abroad.
1949	Twenty-first novel, *The God-Seeker,* published.
1951	Dies of heart disease in Rome on 10 January. Ashes buried in Sauk Centre. Twenty-second novel, *World So Wide,* published posthumously.

LITERARY AND HISTORICAL CONTEXT

1

Historical Background

The history of a nation is only the history of its villages written large.
—Woodrow Wilson, 1900

Carol Kennicott's celebrated revolt from a small Minnesota wheat-town in Sinclair Lewis's *Main Street* (1920) covers about 13 years, mostly the 8 years encompassing her arrival in Gopher Prairie in 1912, her departure in 1918, and her return in 1920. Thus the larger historical events surrounding Carol's youth and maturity in *Main Street* (the sixth of the 22 novels Lewis wrote between 1914 and his death in 1951) correspond precisely to the author's own.

When Harry Sinclair Lewis was born in 1885 his prairie wheat-town—Sauk Centre, Minnesota—still boasted wooden sidewalks, false fronts, hitching posts, iron dogs on lawns, and bewhiskered checker-players. Grover Cleveland presided over 50 million Americans, industrial capitalism drove through the land, and the literary realism in William Dean Howells's *The Rise of Silas Lapham* that year—as in Mark Twain's *Adventures of Huckleberry Finn* the year before—showed itself to fine effect. Eight years later, in 1893, Frederick

Jackson Turner, looking back, publicly read his highly optimistic paper, "The Significance of the Frontier in American History," and Stephen Crane, looking forward, privately issued his highly pessimistic novel, *Maggie: A Girl of the Streets.* Out of the Spanish-American War—in which Lewis tried to enlist at age 13—the United States emerged a first-rate power.

The gawky youth found his hometown, unlike King Arthur's Camelot, dull, ugly, and narrow.[1] "Why don't Doc Lewis make Harry get a job on a farm," he once overheard a neighbor complain, "instead of letting him sit around readin' and readin' a lot of fool histories and God knows what all."[2] Among the "what all" were Balzac and Dickens. From them the boy knew that authors could picture the commonplace, but not until he read Hamlin Garland's *Main-Travelled Roads* (1891) did the bored Yale sophomore, home for the summer of 1905, realize that he could write about the Sauk Centre that he loved and hated. He scribbled in his diary: " 'The village virus'—I shall have to write a book of how it getteth into the veins of a good man & true."[3]

Perhaps because the author of *Main Street* had come of age before the carnage of World War I, he infused into the twentieth-century realism of his five "apprenticeship" novels oodles of nineteenth-century romantic optimism. Lewis's early romances reflect national ideals like heroic individualism, pioneering adventure, middle-class democracy, scientific expansion, and instruments of American promise like the telephone, the automobile, the airplane.

In voyaging to England, the timid little clerk in *Our Mr. Wrenn* (1914) does in reality what rebellious Carol Kennicott only dreams of doing. In *The Trail of the Hawk* (1915) a youth from Joralemon, Minnesota (Carol sees that town in *Main Street* as just another Gopher Prairie), becomes a world-famous aviator. Unlike Una Golden in *The Job* (1917), Dr. Kennicott's wife does not become a successful big-city businesswoman. In Lewis's less "serious" mass-market serial novels, the accent on the positive is even stronger, as when in the flagrantly sentimental *The Innocents* (1917) a merry old couple takes to the open road and in *Free Air* (1919) a western car mechanic convoys a beautiful eastern socialite across the country. Though the second serial is as buoyant as the first, its patches of realism—for example, its grim hamlet of Schoenstrom and its grimy hotel in Gopher Prairie—point directly to *Main Street.*

To his first masterwork, then, Lewis brought not only his episodic method and jittery style, but such popular and personal themes as aspiration, rebellion, and escape. With its genesis in his smoldering "village virus" notation of 1905; its development in his visit to Sauk Centre with his hypercritical wife, Grace Hegger Lewis, in 1916; and its completion in postwar cynicism and disillusionment in 1920, *Main Street* lashes into the outmoded myth of the American small town as altogether honest, friendly, and lovely—as a place untouched by hypocrisy, conformity, and consumerism.

If behind Zona Gale's idealized *Friendship Village* (1908) stand Philip Freneau's "The American Village" (1772) and Timothy Dwight's "Greenfield Hill" (1794), behind Lewis's less than idyllic Gopher Prairie stand such dreary townscapes as Mark Twain's Hadleyburg, E. W. Howe's Twin Mounds, Hamlin Garland's La Crosse, Harold Frederic's Octavius, Edith Wharton's Starkfield, Edgar Lee Master's Spoon River, Willa Cather's Blackhawk, and Sherwood Anderson's Winesburg. Behind Lewis's attack loom social satirists like Voltaire, Shaw, Veblen, Mencken, and, most of all, Mark Twain. And Lewis's full-length portrait of Carol Kennicott brings to mind other male-made leading women characters—in Richardson's *Pamela* (1740), Flaubert's *Madame Bovary* (1865), Tolstoy's *Anna Karénina* (1875–77), Hardy's *Tess of the D'Urbervilles* (1891), Garland's *Rose of Dutcher's Coolly* (1895), and Phillips's *Susan Lenox* (1917).

Thus *Main Street* reflects and illuminates American life, especially for the New Woman of the New Century, under three administrations: Theodore Roosevelt (1901–1909), William Howard Taft (1909–13), and Woodrow Wilson (1913–21). Roosevelt stirred the young to democratize government, battle social injustice, and expose corruption. Revolutionary labor unions and immigrant workers, however, denounced his progressivism as futile. The split in the Republican party gave the Democrats and Wilson's idealist "New Freedom" an overwhelming victory. Promise, however, turned to devastation with America's entrance into World War I in the spring of 1917. The job of caring for millions of veterans after the Armistice fell to the Bureau of War Risk Insurance.

Ambitious young people from isolated farms and backward hamlets flocked to the big cities, the more unconventional and artistic to places like Greenwich Village and the Left Bank. Meanwhile, growing warfare between capital and labor resulted in the Red Scare, in the deportation of aliens, and in the suppression of radicals. No longer able to stand the strain of Wilsonian idealism, American voters (women now as well as men) swept into office handsome Warren G. Harding and his promise of a "return to normalcy." By the end of *Main Street* even Carol Kennicott gives up her job in Washington at the Bureau of War Risk Insurance and returns to the "normalcy" of Gopher Prairie.

By 1920 America was experiencing a revolution in manners and morals. During the decade of bathtub gin and flat-chested shebas in rolled-down hose, Lewis was at his zenith. As the realism in his early novels pointed to *Main Street,* so the panoramic *Main Street* is a trove of themes, types, and social issues that Lewis enlarged upon in his later novels. The middle-aged, middle-class, small-city good citizen in Lewis's next brilliant satire, *Babbitt* (1922), finds business and Rotarian life empty and tries to escape, but, like Carol Kennicott, is drawn back into the fold. The scientist-hero of *Arrowsmith* (1925), however—starting out as a country doctor like Will Kennicott—does break away, first from Wheatsylvania and then, at great cost, from the ignominy of medical commerce. Following the big literary year of 1925, Lewis, refusing and denouncing the Pulitzer Prize, turned out the serial *Mantrap* (1926), a North Woods adventure like nothing Carol Kennicott experiences on her prairie ambles or summer swims. In the heyday of Bible-thumping Billy Sunday and splendiferous Aimee Semple McPherson, *Elmer Gantry* (1927), another major Lewis novel, makes monstrous the slightly ferocious evangelism that Carol encounters in "puritan" Gopher Prairie. The blab of the Babbitt-like monologist in *The Man Who Knew Coolidge* (1928), an amusing jeu d'esprit, is made from the same kind of sounds that booster Jim Blausser makes in *Main Street.* Like the decade itself, Lewis's euphoric roaring ended with *Dodsworth* and the soul-crushing stock-market crash of 1929. The wife that the admirable automobile magnate Sam Dodsworth divorces is affected, faithless, and vicious beyond anything that Dr. Kennicott's rebellious mate can imagine.

Historical Background

The Sinclair Lewis who won the Nobel Prize in 1930 for his satires of the 1920s lost much of his literary force in the decade of the Great Depression. Still, he continued for the rest of his life to poke fun at the crassness of American society. The social consciousness that pricks Carol in *Main Street* becomes in *Ann Vickers* (1933) tedious prison-reform muckraking. Exasperated by literary poseurs and bad hotels (exemplified in *Main Street* by Erik Valborg and the Minniemashie House), Lewis the harassed celebrity and veteran globe-trotter defended inspirational hotel keeping over hack poesy in *Work of Art* (1934). But focusing on a more important issue at the time, demagoguery at home and abroad, Lewis next wrote the propagandistic *It Can't Happen Here* (1935), a frightening magnification of the reactionism that Carol in *Main Street* only hears or reads about. Embraced by the radical Left, the unembraceable Lewis next wrote a weak flipflop novel, *The Prodigal Parents* (1938), with the conservative procreators as heroes and the radical offspring as villains—a sharp turnabout from Carol at the end of *Main Street* pointing to her sleeping daughter as a bomb to blow up future smugness.

As the German war machine swept across Europe, Lewis published his maudlin greasepaint-and-footlights romp, *Bethel Merriday* (1940), on the kind of problems that bedeviled Carol Kennicott as president of the Gopher Prairie Dramatic Association. In 1943, in a period of furious flag-waving and fund-raising, Lewis came forth with *Gideon Planish*, an exposé of organized charity that indeed would frighten the real-life members of small-town do-good clubs like *Main Street*'s Thanatopsis.

After the war, Lewis published *Cass Timberlane* (1945), a novel about Minnesota marriages, centering on a lively young designer and an older judge, which brings to mind young Carol and the memory of her beloved father. At this time African-Americans were pressing for integration, and Lewis, with more anger than art in the improbable *Kingsblood Royal* (1947), attacked the kind of ingrained white discrimination that stirs Carol Kennicott to identify with suppressed nationalities and races. Then, shrugging off social issues and the leading role of the United States in postwar world affairs, Lewis turned instead in *The God-Seeker* (1949) to the pioneering past that so disillusioned Carol Kennicott. By 1950 three-fifths of the 150 million people in America lived in urban areas. In this milieu of television and sonic booms, Woodrow Wilson's definition of a nation's history as the village writ large sounded quaint. As North Korean and other Communist troops drove U.N. forces south of the 38th parallel, Sinclair Lewis lay dying in Rome, far from Sauk Centre. Later that year appeared his posthumous *World So Wide* (1951), its architect-hero's latter-day quest reading like a parody of Carol Kennicott's earlier self-searching. Much fresher seems one of the hurried but happy letters that Lewis wrote to Alfred Harcourt, his publisher, in 1919: "I'll NEVER do a novel more carefully planned and thought out and more eagerly written than *Main Street.*"[4]

2

The Importance of *Main Street*

"If you have it in you," Sinclair Lewis once declared, "to produce one thundering good novel, one really big novel, just one, your place in American literature will be safe for the next hundred years."[5] In *Main Street, Babbitt, Arrowsmith, Elmer Gantry,* and *Dodsworth,* Lewis produced *five* such novels. If literary history has been justly unkind to the bulk (the worst part) of the literary efforts of the American Balzac . . . the American Dickens . . . the American Flaubert, one yet feels safe in assuming that many thousands of students, general readers, and scholars still will experience uncommon pleasure and profit from at least *la crème de la crème—Main Street* and *Babbitt*—well beyond the year 2020.

Exacting critic-biographer Mark Schorer concludes that Sinclair Lewis "unquestionably helped us into the imagination of ourselves as did no other writer of the 1920s."[6] The first explosive novel in the writer's great iconoclastic pentad so shattered the myth of the Midwest as God's Country, of its raw towns as hamlets in Arcady, that the whole revolt-from-the-village tradition in American literature seems even today to have culminated in the remarkable *Main Street,* a novel that has delighted and angered millions of readers around the world.

Like all literary masterpieces, *Main Street* commands attention because it is a locus of values. Critics most often speak of these values in terms of illusion, form, expression, morality. Although some modernists claim that "likeness" (fidelity to actuality) is of little artistic moment, many sophisticated arguments support the idea that art, especially the art of the novel, is essentially an illusion of reality, particularly the reality of people in a social setting. Certainly our sense of *Main Street*'s emphatic locale as a "real" Minnesota wheat-town in the second decade of the twentieth century is telling. In fact, so minute, so accurate, so material seems Gopher Prairie—its dwellings and buildings, its habits and inhabitants—that some readers have gone so far as to judge even the weighty *Middletown* (1929), Robert and Helen Lynd's sociological study of a small American city, as only an extension of the country town in Lewis's trenchant novel.

At times *Main Street*'s verisimilitude indeed resembles a guidebook to the seedy and meretricious or a grammar of sectional slang and immigrant dialect. The novel's memorable "new realism" prompts critics like John F. McCarthy to assert that *Main Street* "remains one of the most magnificently detailed recreations of a bygone era."[7] Comparisons, then, between the fictional Gopher Prairie and the historical Sauk Centre, between Lewis's geoliterary community and small towns familiar to the reader, are inevitable. Although "likeness" is a cardinal novelistic virtue—the one that still matters most to readers today—the serious student will endeavor to judge the ultimate worth of a classic like *Main Street* by more than its distinctive "factual" regionalism, by more than its impressive fidelity to Sauk Centre or some other town.

Readers dwelling only on *Main Street*'s outstanding representational features fail to see the important matter of Carol Kennicott's revolt as a creation, a "making." Even without reference to the urgent world outside *Main Street,* one can appreciate the novel's vital form. While critics seldom fail to point to *Main Street*'s loose plot, its ragged arrangement of events, they consistently shrink from commenting on its noteworthy "architecture." What enables a freewheeling writer like Sinclair Lewis to romp around so gustily in episode after episode is the substantiality of his grand design, a mechanical structure as mathematically proportional, as symmetrically balanced, as a pyramid. With his imposing framework; his notable alternations of realistic, romantic, and satiric modes; his surprising repertoire of narrative techniques; his rhythm of reversals, patterns of images, and system of symbols, Lewis manages to make, in his coarse-grained but electrical prose, a unified whole. Although unity-through-diversity is a paramount artistic value, one should not evaluate the final importance of *Main Street* only on the basis of its varied material, flexible movement, and clever construction.

Because literary art is expression as well as imitation and form, an impulsive writer like Sinclair Lewis endows his inventive recreation with more than the usual degree of personal predilection. As Vernon Parrington once put it: "The family cow, standing knee-deep in June and chewing the cud of contentment, would excite his Diogenic scorn."[8] Through description, exposition, argument, and narration, Lewis consciously and subconsciously, boldly and timidly, categorically and ambivalently expressed in *Main Street* much of his special individuality, his personal makeup, many of his most private feelings, thoughts, and perceptions.

The conventions of satire—irony, burlesque, parody, caricature, sarcasm (and, above all, "unfairness")—doubtless mask some psychic imbalance: Sinclair Lewis's oversystematization and confusion, precision and distortion, folly and genius. Most of his deeper impulses he ventilated in *Main Street* through his satiric narrator, his romantic Carol Kennicott, and his pragmatic Will Kennicott; other spontaneities he discharged through his gallery of tintypes, cartoonish figures that shock us into the kind of recognition we associate today with pop art. Although the expression of emotions, moods, and inner states is central to literary creation, the reader should not determine the ultimate worth of *Main Street* by what it reveals about Sinclair Lewis.

Finally, *Main Street* is the situs of moral value. As the novel embraces truth, beauty, and expression, so it embraces good. "There are paragraphs and single lines," writes Meredith Nicholson, "that arrest the attention and invite rereading, so sharply do they bite into the consciousness."[9] Sinclair Lewis's fictional debunking of the adolescent shortcomings of the bewildered American hinterland was in tune with H. L. Mencken's expository ridicule of *boobus Americanus* for betraying the American Promise by standardizing manners and stultifying morals. In transforming Sauk Centre into Gopher Prairie, Lewis also transfigured Gopher Prairie into the symbol of American provincialism, "its Main Street the continuation of Main Streets everywhere" (6). While *Main Street* mirrors the transition between pre- and post-World War I America, it also reflects the clashing ideas of frontier and postfrontier America.

In idealistic Carol Kennicott flows an important strain of national thought, that peculiar American romanticism stemming from Emerson and Thoreau. But if Carol symbolizes joyous youth rebelling against things-as-they-are (a symbol with wide appeal), she also fits the archetype of the unhappy housewife fleeing hearth and home, a primordial image that also evokes powerful emotions in the reader. Indeed, what makes her story of aspiration, struggle, revolt, and compromise so significant, as she herself realizes, is its articulate protest of "the ordinary life of the age" (422). Still, it would be a mistake to assess *Main Street* only on its "message" or propaganda value, on whether it agrees (or disagrees) with one's own certitudes or with trendy notions on the problem of the individual and the community, freedom and conformity, the one and the many.

That *Main Street* was in its day a cause célèbre, that the very term "Main Street" entered into the American language itself, that Sinclair Lewis became a world figure, that *Main Street* has influenced writers like James T. Farrell, Richard Wright, John Updike, and Philip Roth, that it is an all-time best-seller—these and other such phenomena might well entitle the novel to more than ordinary consideration. But, most important, *Main Street* commands study today because, like all literary masterworks, it remains a rich synthesis of values.

3

Critical Reception

So worried had been Sinclair Lewis about the reception of *Main Street* that while still hammering away at the ending, he urged his publisher, Alfred Harcourt, to send reviewers a letter pointing out the difference between this more serious novel and his earlier fiction. But unlike these earlier efforts, *Main Street* was a literary sensation, welcomed by a cynical postwar generation who liked the idea of tough social criticism, satiric realism, in the garb of fiction. Nearly 300,000 copies of this explosive novel sold the first year, another 100,000 copies before cheaper editions appeared. The time was ripe for *Main Street* to infect millions of readers with its author's diagnosis of the village virus.

Most major reviewers found *Main Street* to have not only an absorbing narrative but sociological significance. Many viewed his mixed genre as pioneering work. Some compared him with Theodore Dreiser and Sherwood Anderson. At least one, believing that Lewis the photographic realist could look below the surface with more than photographic keenness, compared him with Jane Austen and George Eliot. Reviewers commented not only on his sharp eye but also on his sensitive ear, which, they said, could catch and reproduce the sounds of

American vernacular. Besides that, he had his own funny turns of phrase.

Mencken, welcoming Lewis out of the literary hulks, relished *Main Street*'s vivid dialogue, ironic domestic strife, authentic Americanism of character, and, most of all, its packed and brilliant detail. William Allen White, the famous Kansas editor, appreciated Lewis's attack on small-town complacency. William Lyon Phelps of Yale lectured extensively in the East on *Main Street,* Edith Wharton's *Age of Innocence,* and Zona Gale's *Miss Lulu Bett,* all published in 1920. The English writer John Galsworthy thought *Main Street* brilliant, and fellow Minnesotan F. Scott Fitzgerald informed Lewis that *Main Street* had replaced Harold Frederic's *The Damnation of Theron Ware* as his favorite American novel. *Main Street* even interested Ernest Hemingway, perhaps because of his own midwestern boyhood, his doctor father like Will Kennicott, and his cultured mother like Carol.

Still, what most reviewers liked about *Main Street,* others disliked. Some denigrated the form, some the theme, still others the entire enterprise. *Main Street* came under attack for its uneasy mixture of comedy and tragedy, of satire and realism. To be sure, Meredith Nicholson, the author of *The Valley of Democracy*, did not favorably compare *Main Street* with the work of Indiana writers like James Whitcomb Riley and Booth Tarkington. Some reviewers pointed to *Main Street*'s lumpy plot, flat characters, coarse style, and excessive length. For every reviewer who saw Carol's battle with Gopher Prairie as balanced, whole, and hallowed, there was one who saw it as unfair, incomplete, and profane. Interest in the *Main Street* brouhaha spilled over into attention to other recent novels set in small towns, not only Zona Gale's *Miss Lulu Bett* but also Floyd Dell's *Moon-Calf* and Dorothy Canfield's *The Brimming Cup.*

The debate over *Main Street* raged on, spreading to the West and then across the Atlantic. Harcourt and Brace had difficulty keeping bookstores stocked with their runaway best-seller. Even those who had not bothered to read the novel entered the fray. Some folks back in Sauk Centre who saw—or thought they saw—themselves in the novel thought to lynch Good Old Harry. In May, the *New York Times* kept things brewing by publishing two attacks, one on the book and one on the author. The one on the book concluded that its bulky surface detail remained a mystery to the reader; the one on the author denounced him as an "intellectual" who had found fame and fortune by assaulting the American middle class and its established critics.

But idolization continued to run hand-in-hand with excoriation. In June, the *Bookman* gave an account of Harriet Ford and Harvey O'Higgins's forthcoming dramatization of *Main Street. Vanity Fair* nominated Sinclair Lewis to the Hall of Fame for adding the phrase "Main Street" to the spoken language. Although the Pulitzer Prize Committee—Robert Morss Lovett, Stuart Pratt Sherman, and an unenthusiastic Hamlin Garland—chose *Main Street* for its annual novel award, Columbia University ignored the committee vote and presented the 1920 prize to Edith Wharton's brilliant but softer *Age of Innocence.* In July, an Episcopal bishop denounced *Main Street* as a "pagan book," and down in Virginia the Richmond Chamber of Commerce, sensitive to all forms of civic stigma, petitioned the city to change the name of its Main Street. In October, in a widely read article in the *Nation,* "The Revolt from the Village," historian Carl Van Doren lauded Lewis's mimic gusto and placed *Main Street* prominently in the American anti-idyllic literary tradition.

Taking their cue from *Main Street* itself, parodists of all kinds had a field day with the hullabaloo surrounding the book, especially with the thousands of young women enraptured by Carol Kennicott's rebellion. Humorist Carolyn Wells, for example, published *Ptomaine Street* (1921), a clever little blue-and-orange *Main Street* look-alike, starring discontented, puerile Warble Petticoat—hefty spouse of the town's ptomaine specialist—who works herself to thinness trying to reform Butterfly Center, a "plathe" much too addicted to art, beauty, and intellect ever to consider putting up even *one* utilitarian eyesore.

Although Lewis's big novels during the 1920s continued to attract attention and to create controversy, the more genteel critics tended to ignore his work. Still, American writers like Sherwood Anderson, Waldo Frank, Wharton, and Cabell expressed their ideas about Lewis in reviews or essays, as did English writers like Rebecca West, Virginia Woolf, E. M. Forster, and Ford Madox Ford.

Many still viewed *Main Street* as harmful libel, others still looked upon it as beneficial truth. Lewis, of course, identified himself with F. Scott Fitzgerald, Wilbur Daniel Steele, and other members of a "truth-seeking" generation. The first of several promotional booklets on Sinclair Lewis that appeared during the decade came out in 1922. Capitalizing on Lewis's fame and *Main Street*'s popularity, Warner Brothers released a silent film version of the novel, starring Florence Vidor, in 1923. In his *Literary Renaissance in America* that same year, C. H. Bechhofer not only devoted a chapter to the author of *Main Street* but dedicated the whole book to "Sinclair Lewis: Most Romantic of Rebels." One American reviewer referred to one of Knut Hamsun's novels as a "Norwegian *Main Street.*"

The following year Cabell listed in *Straws and Prayer Books* the suggestions that he had made to Lewis for *Main Street,* and Lewis himself wrote an article in the *Nation,* "Main Street's Been Paved," reporting Gopher Prairie's views on the presidential race and its material progress since 1920. Among other characters, Carol Kennicott appears briefly, now a rather dumpy middle-aged woman in spectacles. That year he also boosted Carl Van Vechten's suave attack on provincial Iowa life in *The Tattooed Countess* (1924), but the next year, contrary as ever, he helped journalist Frazer Hunt counter the flood of trendy post-*Main Street* sorties on the American village by endorsing his tendentiously tender novel about an Illinois hamlet, *Sycamore Bend* (1925).

The distinguished literary historian Vernon Parrington hailed Sinclair Lewis as the American Diogenes, but the distinguished satirist Edith Wharton (to whom Lewis had dedicated *Babbitt*) could not bring herself in a *Yale Review* essay to hail *Main Street* as the Great American Novel. A few scholars continued to take up Meredith Nicholson's provillage line, one even contrasting Sinclair Lewis's "sordid" vision with William Allen White's "radiant" one. A social scientist even attempted to measure "social distances" in *Main Street.* But Margaret Anderson, avant-garde editor of the *Little Review,* proclaimed that Sinclair Lewis was naive and that *Main Street* was artless.

Major critics found it difficult (if not impossible) to ignore Sinclair Lewis after he received the Nobel Prize in 1930. In the 1930s doughty literary fellows like Fred Lewis Pattee, V. F. Calverton, Henry Seidel Canby, Christian Gauss, Howard Mumford Jones, and Granville Hicks reviewed Lewis's achievement, endeavoring to locate, or relocate, his niche in American literature, and their assessments of *Main Street* were crucial. Articles on *Main Street* tied the novel to *The Damnation of Theron Ware,* to *Madame Bovary,* and to the Lynds' *Middletown* (1934) and *Middletown in Transition* (1937). Hoping to appeal to moviegoers interested in "women's films," Warner Brothers in 1936 made a sound version of *Main Street,* starring Josephine Hutchinson, but, along with practically everything else, changed the title to the trite *I Married a Doctor.*

During the 1940s Lewis's growing canon, often slipshod and repetitious, came under the scrutiny of a new crop of tough-minded critics like Alfred Kazin, Bernard DeVoto, Maxwell Geismar, and Warren Beck. As always, short pieces on *Main Street,* particularly its setting, continued unabated. Lewis himself noted in 1942 that small-town architecture, especially school buildings, had improved since 1920 (along with merchandising and films), prompting him to wonder if Carol Kennicott's complaints had anything to do with the changes. Still, he could not conceive of his ever again living in Sauk Centre. Other scholarly articles about *Main Street* focused on the novel's ambiguities and on the similarities and differences between Lewis and other writers. In his introduction to a 1946 edition of *Main Street,* Carl Van Doren told of the old furor surrounding the novel's first publication.

A picture story in *Life*, "Main Street 1947," appearing in June of that year, concluded that Sauk Centre was no longer as isolated as it had been in 1920. John T. Flanagan served Lewis scholars well by tracing the roots of *Main Street* to the author's earlier novels. Arguments abounded as to whether *Main Street* was good literature or just good history—or, put another way, good history or mere literature. Some felt that the impact of the one had lost its sting, some that the power of the other had lost its savor. Those who maintained that *Main Street* was not high art were answered by those who believed that Lewis—like Henry Fielding, Daniel Defoe, and Charles Dickens—might well endure longer than the more self-conscious writers and philosophers.

Following Lewis's death in Rome in 1951, scholars and literary critics immediately began arguing about the value of his writings as they reassessed his place in American literature. Meanwhile, the exile's ashes were returned—the irony here is too perfect—to Sauk Centre. The inscription on a simple cemetery marker reads:

Sinclair Lewis, 1885–1951
Author of *Main Street*

No mention is made of the Nobel Prize or of the 21 other novels. Among many others, Alfred Harcourt, James T. Farrell, Frederick Manfred, and Dorothy Thompson paid special tribute. In 1952 Harrison Smith collected Lewis's letters to Harcourt from 1919 to 1930 in *From Main Street to Stockholm,* and in 1953 Harry E. Maule and Melville H. Cane collected some essays in *The Man from Main Street.* In her biographical memoir, *With Love from Gracie* (1955)—a retelling of her novel *Half a Loaf* (1931)—Grace Hegger Lewis sheds additional light on the composition and early celebrity of *Main Street.* In 1955 the *New York Times Magazine* featured a photographic essay on Sauk Centre and the *Saturday Review of Literature* an editorial on the relevance of *Main Street* 35 years later. Mark Schorer in 1958 documented Lewis's ambivalence toward Minnesota. Investigations into the Minnesota background of Lewis's novels and stories continued. Grace Hegger Lewis reminisced in the *New York Times Magazine* about her first visit to Sauk Centre.

The publication of Mark Schorer's massive and impressive official critical biography, *Sinclair Lewis: An American Life* (1961) stimulated renewed interest in the writer and his work. A surprising number of scholars took Schorer to task for what they saw as his failure to grasp his subject's inner life and the nature of his art, but especially disturbing—though understandable—was Schorer's final assessment: "[Lewis] was one of the worst writers in modern American literature, but without his writing one cannot imagine modern American literature" (Schorer 1961, 813). Among the numerous by-products of Schorer's nine-year enterprise were his collection of reviews and essays about Lewis, his afterwords to several Signet Classic reprints, and his three-novel omnibus (*Main Street, Babbitt, Arrowsmith*) appropriately entitled *Lewis at Zenith* (1961).

Other high-quality studies issued from academies around the country. Twayne's United States Authors Series volume on Lewis, by Sheldon Grebstein, appeared in 1962. Journal articles continued to crop up, those on *Main Street* usually stressing the novel's continuing social importance. Several student guides to *Main Street* appeared in the 1960s; and in 1967 D. J. Dooley's defensive *The Art of Sinclair Lewis* was published.

A year later the Minnesota Historical Society designated Sinclair Lewis's boyhood home a historical site. In 1969 Lewis scholar James Lundquist began publishing the short-lived *Sinclair Lewis Newsletter* at St. Cloud State University. The six issues contain a half-dozen interesting articles on *Main Street.* The year also saw the publication of several books on American literature, such as *The Revolt from the Village: 1915-1930* and *The Novelist's America,* with chapters on *Main Street. South Dakota Review* devoted an issue to Manfred and Lewis with two of the articles on *Main Street.* Several shorter biographies, specialized studies, reference guides, and checklists on primary and secondary sources showed up in the 1970s. In *Sinclair Lewis* (1970) James Lundquist explained Lewis's artistry as that of a master of the "popular novel," and in *The Quixotic Vision of Sinclair Lewis* (1975) Martin Light explained the romanticism-realism conflict in Lewis's work. In 1980 came the all-important *Sinclair Lewis: A Reference Guide,* annotated secondary sources published between 1914 and 1978, edited by Robert E. and Esther Fleming.

In a supplement (1979–85) to the Flemings' *Guide,* Robert Fleming in the Sinclair Lewis number of *Modern Fiction Studies* (Autumn 1985) lists eight items on *Main Street*: Hamlin Garland's role in the Pulitzer Prize controversy, the film's subversion of the novel's social criticism, Lewis's attack on the village, his everlasting ambivalence toward Sauk Centre, the affiliation (again) between *Main Street* and *Madame Bovary,* Carol's failure as a new pioneer, her rebellion as a positive act, and, finally, the influence of *Main Street* on Philip Roth's depiction of Lucy Nelson in *When She Was Good* (1967). Not listed is Michael Spindler's Marxist interpretation of

Main Street in *American Literature and Social Change* (1983), wherein Lewis's ambivalence is seen as unsettling and Carol's return to Gopher Prairie as unconvincing. In the issue of the journal itself—edited by Martin Light in honor of Sinclair Lewis's centennial—are two essays, one revealing Carol Kennicott as the model for novelist Nella Larsen's mired black protagonist Helga Crane in *Quicksand* (1928) and the other linking Carol, the pioneering myth, and midwestern bewilderment to Jeffersonian agrarianism, inner freedom, and populist aspiration.

From January to October 1985, the forgiving Sauk Centre celebrated the hundredth birthday of its famous son, with everything from the unveiling of a bronze bust and the issuing of a postage stamp to cake-decorating prizes and snow-sculpture contests. Less commercial and competitive, but with national and local fanfare, St. Cloud State University on 7-9 February hosted a scholarly conference to celebrate the event and to tour nearby Sauk Centre, with its Original Main Street crossing Sinclair Lewis Avenue, its Sinclair Lewis Interpretive Center, its Sinclair Lewis boyhood home, its Sinclair Lewis Park, and so forth.

Twenty-four wide-ranging papers were published under the title *Sinclair Lewis at 100* (1985), with seven focusing on *Main Street.* Two papers compare Lewis's Gopher Prairie with Garrison Keillor's Lake Wobegon, one concluding that Keillor's humor is gentler than Lewis's satire and the other that Gopher Prairie and Lake Wobegon importantly occupy "mythical space." Two papers view Carol from feminist perspectives, one seeing her story as prophetic of contemporary women and the other seeing her as maintaining her integrity and self-worth in spite of her failures. Of the other three papers, one draws parallels between the historical Sauk Centre and Lewis's famous reconstruction in *Main Street,* another suggests the influence of the novel on T. S. Stribling's *Bright Metal* (1928), and the third discusses painter Grant Wood's New Deal interpretation of *Main Street* based on his nine illustrations for a 1936 edition of the novel.

Among other outcomes, the centennial stimulated the republication of James Lundquist's *Sinclair Lewis* in paperback, a small volume of Lewis letters, a PBS television documentary, and my edition of

Critical Essays on Sinclair Lewis (1986), which includes Light's chapter on *Main Street* and Lundquist's original essay, based on his examination of local newspapers of the 1890s, about the terrifying Sauk Centre that the novelist did not write about, thus enabling the student to discern Sinclair Lewis's "unacknowledged background of horror."

Other essays on *Main Street* during the 1980s take up discussions of Lewis as a social diagnostician, of *Main Street* as a complement to the sociology of small towns, of Lewis as sympathetic to the plight of modern women, and of Lewis and Keillor as close in space but far in time and sensibility. In 1987 Harold Bloom edited a highly selective volume of essays in his Modern Critical Views Series, which reprints a few essays touching on *Main Street.* In 1990 newspaperwoman Roberta Olson of Sauk Centre published a little book, *Sinclair Lewis: The Journey,* on Lewis's career and relation to Sauk Centre. A group of scholars founded the Sinclair Lewis Society at the 1992 meeting of the American Literature Association, and later that year the Library of America published a one-volume edition of *Main Street & Babbitt* in its series Literary Classics of the United States. Thus a surprising number of scholars and students still find Sinclair Lewis a strangely compelling figure in American literature and *Main Street* a strangely compelling book.

Obviously, no reading of *Main Street* can exhaust intelligent discussion about the countless little creative acts that go into making a great book. Still, the reception of *Main Street* into this Masterwork Series format allows for a reading at least commensurate with the novel's complexity and scope. Most helpful to such a reading have been the best critical insights arising from the debate over *Main Street* since 1920. These treat the revolt-from-the-village tradition, the reading of *Main Street* as literature and as history, the sociological and satiric importance of the novel, its odd ambivalence, the romanticism-realism dilemma, the problem of freedom and bewilderment, and the nature of Carol's rebellion and return. Least helpful to the debate have been extremist sentiments, ranging from sweeping denunciations of *Main Street* as a vilification of the small town and American womanhood to wholesale declarations of the novel as the last word on little communities and the American housewife. The passion surrounding the early excoriation and idolization of *Main Street* has long been spent. Today we can enjoy the novel with a large measure of detached recognition. My concern here is to read it as a compelling work of the literary imagination.

Particularly suitable to a long, loose-jointed work like *Main Street* is a combined approach. As this reading follows the larger design of the narrative (Carol's various roles during the course of her story), it also groups and examines recurring themes, motifs, and techniques. Thus it focuses on the present, past, and future of Gopher Prairie and of Carol Kennicott; on the conflict of the mind and body of the one with the spirit and substance of the other; on their dreams and aspirations, their satisfactions and discontents, their honesties and hypocrisies; on issues in education, religion, politics, and literature; on Lewis's intrusive narrator, slashing satire, and relentless cataloging; on his orchestration of motifs like high and low, entrapment and escape, effervescence and death. Such a reading helps us see more clearly the figure in the spacious carpet—the revolt of Carol Kennicott against Main Street.

A READING

4

Prairie Princess

Main Street is too episodic and improvisational to be called a "well-made" novel. Still, Sinclair Lewis's anatomy of a small town has formal interest. The underlying structure, for example, is not only proportional but symmetrical. The novel's 39 chapters, an accumulation of long and short scenes teeming with detail, divide neatly into seven parts. But because the author does not block off or signal these larger units or centers of interest distinctly, the novel's overall design might seem, like some chapters, misshapen.

Of the seven tacit parts, three (six chapters each) lead into a three-chapter centerpiece; three parts (six chapters each) follow it. The first of the seven larger units or sections introduces the reader to Carol Milford, first as a college student, next as a St. Paul librarian, and finally as Dr. Will Kennicott's bride. The second part describes Carol Kennicott's struggles to fit into philistine Gopher Prairie. The third describes her trials, first as helpmate to her husband and then as director of an amateur play. The centerpiece, part four, depicts Carol as a semisatisfied young mother. The fifth section shows her increasing estrangement from her husband and her intellectual revolt from Gopher Prairie. The sixth part treats Carol Kennicott's involvement with young Erik Valborg. And the last, the seventh, details her physical revolt from the village and, after nearly two years with her son in Washington, D.C., her return.

More specifically, the first six-chapter section characterizes quixotic Carol Milford as an undergraduate in St. Paul and as a graduate student in Chicago; describes her work with the St. Paul Public Library and her romance with Will Kennicott; details the couple's trip to Gopher Prairie following their Colorado honeymoon; reveals the young bride's impressions and ambivalence toward wedlock and small-town life; and finally depicts Carol's elaborate housewarming party.

Time in chapter 1 moves rapidly, from 1907 to 1911, from the college senior to the disenchanted librarian. The reader first sees young Carol Milford, whose moods move the plot of *Main Street,* as a rebellious college idealist alone on a hilltop. One of her sundry dreams, to make beautiful an ugly prairie village, foreshadows her later conflict with Gopher Prairie. Carol's various goals, Lewis makes clear, derive from her sense of superiority. Deciding on a career in library science, she foresees herself as a distinguished scholar. Lewis intensifies Carol's early devotion to her ideals by having her reject marriage. And by placing Carol in Chicago as a graduate student, he heightens her sophistication while clouding some of her illusions about *la vie de bohème.*

Weary Carol Milford then meets virile Will Kennicott. Chapter 2 details their meeting and summarizes their year-long courtship. The third chapter, where a Jamesian or "well-wrought" novel might start, brilliantly renders Dr. and Mrs. Will Kennicott's reeky train trip to Gopher Prairie in the fall of 1912. Revolted by the town's ugliness, dazed by Will's welcoming friends, and oppressed by the Kennicott house, Carol in chapter 4 yet aspires to make them all her own. Although before her marriage Carol had wanted to see Gopher Prairie—the run from St. Paul is short and Will's courtship long—Lewis dramatically but improbably has Carol first lay eyes on the place after her marriage. Here Carol makes her famous 32-minute walk through the dreary town.

To illustrate the relativity of values, Lewis heavy-handedly pictures the simultaneous arrival of Bea Sorenson, a farmgirl thrilled by Gopher Prairie's cosmopolitanism. The chapter ends with Lewis's notable scene of the Clarks' welcoming party. Chapter 5 moves from the sublime to the ridiculous, from Carol's tramping over the placid prairie the next day with Will to her "culturine" boardinghouse chatter with Raymie Wutherspoon. The author follows up his parody of hyperbolic small-town newspapers with Carol's tribulations, first with nosey Mrs. Bogart and then with household finance. Carol "effervesces anew," however, as she painstakingly prepares for her "Oriental" housewarming party, which she imagines will awaken the town to new heights of merrymaking. Again, Lewis parodies the *Dauntless*'s puffy reporting of Carol's festive originality. The first part of *Main Street* ends, ironically enough, with Gopher Prairie falling back the following week into its accustomed social grooves.

The story of Carol Kennicott comes to the reader from a third-person omniscient point of view. That is, most of what we read is from Carol's perspective, but much also comes from other perspectives, particularly from Lewis's alter ego or intrusive novelist-narrator, who, no mere fly on the wall, chattily confides to the reader what Carol knows, sees, thinks, and feels, as well as what she does not know, see, think, and feel. To render his undergraduate's innocence, for example, the sapient narrator affirms: "She did not yet know the immense ability of the world to be casually cruel and proudly dull; but if she should ever learn these dismaying powers, her eyes would never become sullen or rheumily amorous" (8). Again, when rejected classmate Stewart Snyder puts to Carol that eternal male question to the restless female—What is better than home, family, and friends?—the freewheeling narrator waggishly poeticizes: "Thus to the young Sappho spake the melon-vendors; thus the captains to Zenobia; and in the damp cave over gnawed bones the hairy suitor thus protested to the woman advocate of matriarchy" (15). The narrator assures us that however collegiate Carol's idiom, the voice is Sappho's.

When reporting the flirtation between Will and Carol, he impishly dispels the note of Tennysonian medievalism that he himself sounds: "Thus in the Vale of Arcady nymph and satyr beguiled the hours; precisely thus, and not in honeyed pentameters discoursed Elaine and the worn Sir Launcelot in the pleached alley" (18). When

Lewis chooses to detail or dramatize an element of plot, he becomes brazenly reticent. Of the Chicago studio party, he explains: "It cannot be reported that Carol had anything significant to say to the Bohemians" (15). As for the doctor's year-long courtship of the librarian: "Of the love-making of Carol and Will Kennicott there is nothing to be told which may not be heard on every summer evening, on every shadowy block" (20).

More effective are the novelist's rich details, as in his description of the train to Gopher Prairie; not until the second section of chapter 3 does the narrator reveal the presence on board of Dr. and Mrs. Will Kennicott. The juxtaposition here between descriptive vignette and storyline resembles John Steinbeck's later intercalary chapters in *The Grapes of Wrath* (1939). As for Carol's first walk down Main Street, the narrator assures us that "In supposing that only she was observant Carol was ignorant, misled by the indifference of cities" (36). The point of view shifts readily from inner to outer world: "She was within ten minutes beholding not only the heart of a place called Gopher Prairie, but ten thousand towns from Albany to San Diego" (38). Other notable intrusions in part one of *Main Street* are the narrator's readerly introductions of Vida Sherwin and the Widow Bogart—the one as energetic as a chipmunk, the other as mushy as a fricasseed chicken with dumplings.

Most of the 80 or more characters in *Main Street* are caricatured, like the Widow Bogart, or artfully simplified, like Vida Sherwin. No one else in the novel, at any rate, is as complexly discontented as Carol or as intricately complacent as Will. Hard at work in *Main Street* is not only Lewis's mix of narrative, scene, and dialogue but also his special blend of wit and criticism—his highly energetic, highly effective, satire. Critic Mark Schorer notes rightly in his afterword to the Signet Classic *Main Street* that Lewis distributes his satire unevenly, but surely he is mistaken when he states that the satire in the novel does not begin until Carol Kennicott looks for the first time in chapter 4 into Ludelmeyer's grocery store window (437).

The one-page untitled prologue to *Main Street* is itself a microcosm of raillery as, pleading between the lines for reader sympathy, it pricks American small-town pride in its Fords, Bon Tons, and

Rosebuds—in the opinion of its shopkeepers and in the wisdom of its bankers. *Blodgett,* the garishly consonantal name of Carol's alma mater, assails the eye and ear, bringing to mind Mark Twain's sham Dauphin, who in *Adventures of Huckleberry Finn* introduces himself to a country jake as "Blodgett—Elexander Blodgett—*Reverend* Elexander Blodgett, I spose I must say, as I'm one o' the Lord's poor servants." Over Blodgett's gymnasium floor "hulking young women" in blue bloomers "thuddingly galloped" (8). The abode of Blodgett's president, even with its stuffy portraits of John Greenleaf Whittier and Martha Washington, resembles a funeral home; inevitably, the school orchestra plays *Carmen* and *Madame Butterfly.* Paradoxically, many a betrothed coed pretends that an important job awaits her, while many a job seeker feigns having a fabulous suitor. Finally, Lewis pokes fun at the studio party Carol attends in Chicago. Thus Lewis fairly paves his satiric road by the time Carol, looking into Ludelmeyer's grocery window, sees "dubious pumpkins" (36).

Also dubious are Carol's own opinions on burning issues; but so one-sided and self-condemnatory does the author-as-caricaturist make the vernacular excesses, the cartoonlike balloons over the heads of so many Gopher Prairieites, that Lewis encourages the reader to take, if not Carol's view, at least some opposing line, as when, for example, "Professor" George Edwin Mott (school superintendent) holds forth on local education, Jackson Elder (mill owner) on local unions, Raymie Wutherspoon (shoe salesman) on local culture, and the *Dauntless* (village weekly) on local news. Again, one recognizes the mimetic tradition of Mark Twain. Though often ludicrous, Lewis's dated Americanese is effectively grounded in experience.

If *Main Street*'s length, digressions, exaggerations, and bardic narrator remind us of the epic, so too does its array of catalogs. Even as an aspiring young writer, sharp-eyed Lewis nailed down his wholesale observations in notes for later use. His lists of persons, places, and things call up Homer's *katalogos* of ships in the *Iliad* or Milton's register of fallen angels in *Paradise Lost.* In this first section of *Main Street,* Lewis catalogs Blodgett dormitory decor, Bohemian chatter, Gopher Prairie paragons, Will's hometown snapshots, a train car and its passengers (down to the contents of a young mother's suitcase), Main

Street sights, the Clarks' furnishings, Pete Rustad's farm, and, finally, village sounds. As with his pictures of the urban scene, Lewis inundates even rural America with material things. As he later wrote in his introduction to David Cohn's *The Good Old Days* (1940)—a study of Sears, Roebuck catalogs—"by your eyebrow pencils, your encyclopedias, and your alarm clocks shall ye be known."[10]

Known to us from the beginning as a romantic dreamer, Carol naturally and conventionally gravitates to soul-stirring heights. Even as a child in Mankato, she would climb the banks of the Minnesota River and "listen" to its fables. Thus by way of images and metaphors of height throughout *Main Street,* Lewis conveys not only Carol's idealism and pride but also his own glorification of youthful aspiration. Standing in the opening scene like a harp in the wind on a Minnesota hilltop overlooking the Mississippi and the world so wide, the optimistic and rebellious college girl symbolizes for the fabulist Lewis "suspended freedom," "the eternal aching comedy of expectant youth," "the spirit of that bewildered empire called the American Middlewest" (7-8).

As she contemplates her benevolent conquest of the world, Carol, for all her generous feeling, is "gently aloof and critical." Naively imagining herself a high-minded liberator ("I just love common workmen" [10]), she can yet feel marvelously humbled when told that common workmen don't think they're common. Still, from her imagined holy high place, she yearns to reach down, to inspire people, to improve the "grateful poor" (11), to beautify a prairie town. Even when part of the crowd, Carol instinctively stands above, observing and wondering. Simply put, this high-flying rebel wants "everything in the world" (15).

In St. Paul, the wage earner is proud of her fellow librarians' expectations, but she also realizes that she is not heightening lives. Her patrons want no "elevated essays" (16). Greeted by Will as a "high mogul" in the library system (18), she confides that she likes to view the cliffs and farms from Summit Avenue. Later she tramps with Will across the High Bridge and in "delicious imaginary fear" gazes down at the "Yang-tse village of St. Paul mud flats" (21). But truly stuck in the mire to the transcendental bride—she who with rising blood and rising sap pitched her honeymoon tent high in the Colorado Rockies—are the Gopher State farmers on the train. Soon, from a climbing railroad curve, she looks down and sees the whole flatness of Gopher Prairie.

Later, hoping to glimpse something of village charm below her "boudoir" window (35), Carol sees instead a little catalog of scenic horrors. Only at the end of this first section, at her housewarming, do we see Carol's dream of elevation realized. As she had looked down on her Orientalized St. Paul from the High Bridge, so from the top of the stairs she looks down on her Orientalized Gopher Prairieites and inanely sings out: "The Princess Winky Poo salutes her court!" (80).

In a novel crowded with details, Lewis assigns surprisingly few to the face and figure of his prairie princess. Like Dreiser's Carrie Meeber, Lewis's Carrie Milford is very pretty. Most important, Carol's "ingénue" eyes are intense, observing, questioning (8). Noteworthy are her anomalies. Her hair ("black glass") is in the tradition of the dark passionate lady (15), while her skin ("quince-blossom") is the prescription for the fair virginal damsel (8). Again, as the ambition of thin-wristed, thin-shouldered Carol is beyond her strength, so her vitality alone magnifies her "gay white littleness" (45). To Will's discomfort, his young wife not only alludes to her ankles in public (in a day—1912—when such allusion was risqué), but she playfully displays them.

To heighten his heroine's aplomb, Lewis makes Carol Milford an orphan, unshielded except for the aegis of Blodgett and the advice of her older, married, "vanilla-flavored" sister (9). The Milfords of Mankato, Minnesota, explains the narrator, had been an ingeniously self-sustaining family, with the kindly and learned paterfamilias, a judge from Massachusetts, nimble at playing the hearth mythologist and at creating wacky "dressing-up parties" (12). As a Sauk Centre boy, Harry Sinclair Lewis, like Carrie Milford, had a passion for costumes. "Masquerading," writes biographer Mark Schorer, "was apparently the earliest form taken by that lifelong propensity for mimicry that was both to make [Lewis] famous and to bore his friends" (Schorer 1961, 31).

Carol's vivid memories of her joyously rumpled sire, a quietly persistent motif in *Main Street,* contribute to her development, to many of her actions, standards, and directions. One discerns something of Judge Milford's New England heritage in his hero-worshipping daughter: Emerson's idealism, Thoreau's natural world, Hawthorne's picturesqueness, Longfellow's Old Europe, and Brook Farm's utopianism. Lewis himself, particularly as an undergraduate in his father's Connecticut, responded powerfully to the literary giants of nineteenth-century New England, especially (so he later claimed) to Thoreau, who not only revolted against the materialistic complacency of Concord village but visited Minnesota in 1861.

While Carol, too, revolts against crass materialism, obviously she would not take seriously Thoreau's dictum to beware of all enterprises that require new clothes. Her eye for fashion is largely the eye of Grace Hegger Lewis. One assumes that Carol's clothes-consciousness began in the good old days of her father's stagey diversions. The collegian's flairing taffeta, at any rate, capitulates to the librarian's blue serge. On the train an approving Will refers to his bride's blue negligee as a "vampire costume" (28); in the Victorian bedroom of the Kennicott house, however, Carol feels that her lacy black chemise is so out of place that she hides it under a "sensible linen blouse" (36). Ironically, grocer Ludelmeyer views Mrs. Kennicott's gray suit as too plain even for Main Street. Again, the arriviste feels that her low-throated slip of lawn and gold sash is so inappropriate at the Clarks' gathering that she speciously oscillates between the spinsterish and the rebellious. At her own housewarming, however, Carol settles on appearing first in a "silver sheath" (75)—one recalls the violinist's "straight golden" (9) directoire silhouette at Blodgett—followed by a change into her party-stealing Chinese "dress-up"—trousers and a coat of silver brocade.

Changing, moving freely in all directions, Carol is a victim of her own "perilous versatility" (8). Her experiments at Blodgett College (tennis, partying, male friends, art, music, drama, social clubs, and charity work) all resurface in the course of this long novel. Upon discovering her lack of genius in one area, she either takes up subordinate work or finds another field of interest. "Always she was disappointed, but always she effervesced anew" (9). She relates her experimental and partial successes to an array of possible callings: lawyer, film writer, nurse, teacher, town planner, dancer, wife of a hero. On advice from an English professor, she settles on librarianship as a way "to do something with life" (14). Because she loves the scenic, she accompanies Will on his shooting walks as easily as she stalks "General Culture" (8). This trick of capitalization Lewis might have picked up from George Ade's racy *Fables in Slang* (1899). Eager to try different recipes, she shops for certain foods, even after she discovers Main Street's gastronomic limitations and hires droll Bea Sorenson as cook. Carol's dexterity is as evident as her dislike for dishwashing.

Part and parcel of Carol's aloofness, whether natural or cultivated or both, is her sympathy, her desire in college to "mother" the world. Upon graduation, she regrets not knowing all her classmates intimately. In Dr. Will Kennicott's profession she sees "such an opportunity for sympathy" (19). His photos of Gopher Prairie and of a farm baby play on Carol's feelings. Her compassion for the farmers on the train is uncomfortably acute. Though crude manners repulse her, she wants to like the people her husband likes. Playing the Clever Little Bride from the Cities, she shines exhibitionistically at the Clarks'. At Pete Rustad's farm she finds Helga Rustad endearing. At Mrs. Gurrey's boardinghouse she urges Raymie Wutherspoon to hold forth on the cultural scene. On Main Street she hails the other housewives, chats with a girl, parleys with a boy. Out in the country she visits Will's patients. At her own housewarming Carol even predisposes herself to delight in Raymie's saccharine recital.

Carol's predisposition to sympathize is often at odds with her predisposition, even if self-deluded, to be frank, to despise lying—both in herself and in others. One wonders if she really has heard, as she is moved to tell Will upon first meeting him, that Gopher Prairie is a "nice town" (19). Experiencing a less than rosy entrance into her new life on the prairie, she wonders: "Why do these stories lie so?" (33). When Will checks into his office so soon after their arrival in Gopher Prairie, Carol pretends not to be disappointed, as she pretends again after Will asks how she liked her first walk down Main Street. Here the narrator sympathetically interprets Carol's "very interesting" as "self-protective maturity" (41). Her bolder lie to Juanita Haydock—that she plays bezique but not bridge—jolts us into realizing just how much Carol Kennicott wants both to impress and to sympathize with Gopher Prairie.

The clash between Carol Kennicott and Gopher Prairie stems from the claims of the imagination and the claims of the world. Her early quixotism paves the way for her unreachable dreams in Gopher Prairie. A questioner, she is also credulous, romanticizing not only her sociology instructor but her field trip into penury as she youthfully envisages herself a secular nun in a settlement house, a cultural avant-gardist, a planner of "darling" villages, an uplifting librarian, a celebrated scholar (11). To accent Carol's capriciousness, even as a graduate student, Lewis quips that in Chicago she almost abdicated library work to become "one of the young women who dance in cheese-cloth in the moonlight" (15). Even as a librarian in St. Paul, Carol reverberates to her dream of planning a quaint town. On the train to Gopher Prairie she swings between exuberance and depression. At times she views the prairie as empty and threatening, at other times as glorious and majestic—perceptions found in the writings of Frank Norris and Willa Cather. But soon the distant lakes, divested of Carol's idealization, simply resemble Will's snapshots. Still, the bride, flinging up the window, places her hand theatrically on her breast and soulfully expresses the wonder of archetypal arrival.

Although the Milford hearth mythology was too innocent for night animals—with Lewis/Carol's "ferriginous" and "skitama regg" out of Lewis Carroll's "slithy toves" and "borogoves"—the judge's daughter, bizarrely enough, sees the old pieces of Kennicott furniture as condemning judges. Main Street, too, induces wonder and disillusion. At the Clarks' party Carol enacts earlier imaginings of herself as a chic spouse fencing conversationally with clever men. On the prairie she transforms her husband into Great Hunter, at the Rustad farm into Lord of the Manor. As Clever Little Bride, Carol self-consciously plays house, parades to market, and mock-quarrels with Dave Dyer, the druggist. As back at the Blodgett reception she imagined the palms as jungle, the light as haze, and the faculty as Olympians, so at her fantastic "Chinese" housewarming she imagines Guy Pollock and herself roaming on an island in a yellow sea of chatter.

Afflicted with "wonderlust" (60), Carol is also drawn to advanced ideas like iron filings to a magnet. She esteems learning, eschews anti-intellectualism. At the Clarks', she asks Superintendent Mott about educational experiments. But pedagogic sophistication, Carol quickly senses, is no substitute in Main Street society for ignorance of bridge. Bored by women's gossip, Carol quickly discovers that the men also talk chaff. Just when Carol needs a bookmate, Lewis contrives to have Vida Sherwin call. Even though their literary tastes diverge, Carol relishes her colloquy with Vida. From the schoolteacher's enthusiastic report, Carol gathers, quite rightly, that the Thanatopsis Club is not intellectually exhilarating. Why does a highly intelligent man like Guy Pollock, Carol wonders, remain in Gopher Prairie, a town that has lost the power of impersonal thought as well as of play?

In addition to forming her trio of Gopher Prairie Illuminati—Carol, Vida, and Guy—intellectual ringleader Carol is alive to physical sensations: dancing, walnut fudge, satin pillows, male strength, comely children, outdoor beauty. But compared with her Colorado honeymoon, the bride's erotic life in Gopher Prairie seems cramped. Her very approach to the flat prairie town dims her ardor. Striking a blow for reticence and "best-laid plans," Lewis resorts to sexual symbolism and ellipsis as the couple enters the empty house: "She jiggled while he turned the key, and scampered in. . . . It was next day before either of them remembered that in their honeymoon camp they had planned that he should carry her over the sill" (34). The narrator then abruptly shifts the reader back to the couple's entrance. In the dingy, airless parlor, Carol slips her hands beneath Will's coat, her fingers over the back of his satin waistcoat. She seems "almost to creep into his body" (34). But suddenly, with Will gone for a quick visit to his office, Carol, in the bedroom, pronounces her lacy black chemise a "hussy" (35), and then takes her walk down Main Street. Returning from the Clarks' party that evening, Will, in the best popular-fiction manner, does indeed lift Carol and, her arms about his neck, does ritualistically carry her over the sill and into the house. But the delay makes the act seem less genuine, less logical and credible.

Besides discovering the honeymoon joys of full-bodied sexual feelings in the untrammeled Rockies, Carol delights in local outdoor excitements. With her appetite for color and form, she views the countryside, in fact, as superior to the town as she and Will amble over the serene prairie. She sees his hunting gear as something "creative and joyous" (57), his gun and shells as art objects.

With much less interest in hunting and fishing than Will, Sinclair Lewis endows Carol—a sort of Leatherstocking Bluestocking—with his own penchant for hiking and observing the great outdoors. His thumbnail sketch of the little woods—birches, poplars, and circle lake—reads like a passage out of *Walden.* "Carol had found the dignity and greatness which had failed her in Main Street" (61).

Though back at Blodgett Stewart Snyder had painted Carol an inviting picture of Yankton picnicking, sleighing, and fishing, she rejects his marriage proposal, telling him that she does not understand herself. Still, Carol does examine her feelings, often with insight into her limitations and self-irony about her situation. She realizes, for example, her disdain for routine and her deference to extravagance, both by-products of her castle building. Though at times she pronounces as "ludicrous" her dream of village beautification, she remains a self-styled town planner. While humoring Raymie Wutherspoon at the boardinghouse, Carol confesses to a lack of humor; indeed, her caprices are more melancholy than sanguine. She is well aware of her flightiness, silliness, nervousness, restlessness, oversensitiveness, instability, and even hysteria.

Yet, from the opening hilltop scene, Sinclair Lewis strikes the note of Carol's attractiveness to men. Theatrically, the author has some passerby gazing up wistfully at the windblown girl as she, unaware of this "chance watcher" (7), recollects the professor who had stared at her new coiffure. To emphasize further Carol's touch of unconventionality and allure, the narrator hyperbolically reports that in chapel every man witness to Carol as angelic violinist fell in love with her and with religion. Her fragility is protected most particularly by robust coeds and by amorous lawyer-to-be Stewart Snyder. Though averse to routine, Carol never seems bored by her string of St. Paul knights. Only resolute Sir Will, however, drawn to her finesse, emerges from the lists victorious. As his charming bride, Carol easily conquers friendly Sam Clark and puppy-eyed Raymie Wutherspoon. As Chinese princess at her housewarming, she senses in both Will and Guy a "hunger" for her (80). Thus in little humdrum Gopher Prairie Sinclair Lewis makes his readers aware of the potential for romantic triangles and sexual intrigue.

The "hunger" that Carol Kennicott senses indeed gratifies her. And the popularity, admiration, and recognition that she, graceful and pretty, desires is the same popularity, admiration, and recognition that Lewis, gawky and homely, yearned for. Carol admires the Marburys of St. Paul largely because they admire her. Will's adoration of Carol is as conspicuous, if not as inventive, as Lewis's for Grace Hegger. When Sam Clark gallantly declares that Will's bride is the "prettiest *Frau*" in Gopher Prairie, Carol thinks, "I shall like Mr. Clark" (32). As much as Sinclair Lewis playing Life of the Party, Carol strains for stardom by playing Clever Little Bride from the Cities; but when Will later hints at a lack of decorum at her party, she wonders if Gopher Prairie was laughing *at* her. Effervescing anew, however, she feels that even the shopkeepers treat her as a personage. The impact of her refurbished living room on her guests tickles her vanity. She savors their looking up in a "suspense of admiration" at her royal self (80). To keep their fealty, she suppresses as too obscene for Main Street her impulse to impress them even further by lighting a cigarette. When Will again cautions her, this time about showing her knees, she displays a pique soothed only by the company's complimenting her on "the nicest party they'd ever seen" (81).

Carol, after all, is rebelling against Mrs. Grundy and Main Street's restrictive past. One recalls that on her breezy hilltop Carol Milford thinks not of Chippewa clans or Yankee traders. Still, after the narrator asserts that the early days of pioneering are "deader" now than Camelot (7), he yet characterizes the restlessness both of Carol and "the Cities" as extensions of the pioneering spirit. History for the Carol who had listened to the river's fables is less classroom chronicle than flickering images. Will and Carol's visit to shrines of the westward movement, Sibley House and old Fort Snelling, connect them with other days. Sentimental it might be, but Lewis has them talking more freely and proudly, deeming themselves inheritors of the American Dream. From this high and mythic vantage above the marriage of the Mississippi and the Minnesota, the country doctor begs the city librarian to come to Gopher Prairie.

Carol, who carries Camelot within, discovers on her bewildering trip to Gopher Prairie that for all the fat richness of the Midwest, it is still a pioneer land, full of sweaty wayfarers and ugly settlements, and that her new home seems to her closer to a frontier mining camp than to a civilized community. Even so, she views the town's contemporary saloon vice as "feeble and unenterprising and dull" (38). Since Carol at this time really knows neither Gopher Prairie's past nor its present, her radiant plans rest on severe limitations.

Measured by Mankato, Venice, and Camelot, Gopher Prairie indeed is found wanting. Carol looks upon Will's hometown—and America has 10,000 Gopher Prairies—as a "junk-heap" (33), the romantic's naturalistic shock of recognition. When she first recalls in St. Paul that Gopher Prairie is a Minnesota "wheat-prairie town of something over three thousand" (18) the reader already divines Carol's future. Though the town is not "artistic," declares Will, its trees, lakes, and cement walks make it "darn pretty" (19). He invites Carol to improve it. Thus begins Lewis's ambivalent attack-report-defense of small-town America. Carol's feelings about the bleak railroad settlements prefigure her feelings about Gopher Prairie, a setting that appeared earlier in Lewis's story "A Rose for Little Eva" in 1918 and briefly in *Free Air* a year later. She sees the town as simply an "enlargement" of a settlement (30), a perfect word in light of Will's seductive snapshot-show. Aesthetic-minded and critical Carol is overwhelmed by the ugliness, straightness, and planlessness of this pig in a poke. Its frame houses, grain elevators, meek cottages, church steeples, and new bungalows seem to her dull symbols of prosperity. "Each man had built with the most valiant disregard of all the others" (41).

So explosive is Carol's first impression of Main Street that it remains with the reader throughout the novel, even though the author pictures little more of downtown Gopher Prairie. On all sides the prairie threatens the low brick shops and wooden houses, in front of which stand Fords and lumber wagons. Conspicuously absent for the judge's daughter is a courthouse, as well as a lovely park. Ugly to Carol are the shabby hotel, the greasy drugstore, an unsanitary grocery, the reeking meat market, a crude general store, a Greek candy store, the barbershop-and-poolhall, the unimaginative furniture store, a greasy restaurant, a dreary clothing store, a broken jeweler's clock, stale saloons, sour-smelling warehouses, and a roaring garage. (Will's office window over the drugstore resembles the Sauk Centre office of Lewis's father, Dr. Edwin J. Lewis.) The slapstick in the Rosebud Movie Palace, the pornography in the Smoke House, and the kitsch in Ye Olde Art Shoppe cater to depressed tastes. Only the Bon Ton Store, the State Bank, and the Farmers' National Bank offer aesthetic relief.

Across Carol's path pass all the types and classes of Gopher Prairie society. Before her arrival, Carol had only Will's imparted view: Gopher Prairieites lack "finesse," but they are the "best" people on earth (22). Their welcoming friendliness comes in the synecdotic form of coarse voices, damp hands, bald spots. On her private tour of Main Street, she beholds the uncomely natives: a yawner with pink arm-garters, farmwives waiting in wagons in front of saloons for their bellowing husbands, surly garagemen, a toothpick-sucker, a barber in shirt-sleeves, a farmer dirty and unshaved, staring young loafers.

Lewis illustrates the reality of class in America when he depicts a higher grade of citizen gracing Sam Clark's party as they sit in a circle and stare at Carol. For 15 minutes she amuses them, but these representatives of the hunting, educational, and financial sets do not, in turn, amuse her. Soon the men and women divide for gossip and shoptalk. After the old stunts, the old coma sets in. The boardinghouse crowd, Carol notes, chew like horses. But through the rosy-colored lenses of a new arrival, she looks upon merchants as confidants, and she appreciates the squatting elders and the beautiful children. In the best Gopher Prairie manner, the customary circle forms even at Carol's housewarming, and after the time-to-leave coughs the guests compliment her on her cleverness and originality.

Besides loathing Will's "darn pretty town" and many of its denizens, Carol hates the old damp brown cube of a Kennicott house on Poplar Street. Will, however, sees it as "nice and roomy" (33). As far as Carol is concerned, its first-rate furnace in no way compensates for its scrolls and brackets, lugubrious bay window, cheap lace curtains, pink and marble table, and other stuffy Victoriana. The dismal

L-shaped bedroom (with its black walnut bed, imitation maple bureau, and gewgaws) makes Carol shudder. In an effort to be economical and yet bring her little gods of the hearth into the house, Carol shops in Minneapolis for golden pillows and a yellow-and-blue Japanese obi against which she hangs a vermilion print. Since Will plans to build a new house in a few years, she redecorates only the one room. Though Carol's furniture is too queer and subtle for Gopher Prairie, the Japanese taste of the time was already a cliché in middle-class cities and suburban homes.

Carol's wish to tutor Gopher Prairie in the tenuous matter of taste, to be its *arbiter elegantarium,* contributes to the novel's more general theme of American education. While Sinclair Lewis promoted reading and the diffusion of knowledge, he abhorred the hours pilfered from lively youth by dull educationists. Carol's history class at Blodgett is Lewis's case in point. While religiously protected from university wickedness by Blodgett's tight little campus, Carol yet experiments. Like many of the relatively few female college graduates of her day, Carol yearns to use her education for the good of the world. Were she to become a school teacher, she believes that, unlike the piously earnest, she would never be insincere or dreary or sarcastic. Most of all, she'd never simply drone facts to unwilling students. But Carol also realizes, to her credit, that she could never endure pedagogic routine and grinning children. Ironically, Will, in effect, invites Carol to educate Gopher Prairie. When she asks Superintendent Mott about educational experiments, Lewis's satire is implicit, as noted, in Mott's mossback response. Initially, however, energetic Vida Sherwin, remarking on her own teaching rut, invites Carol Kennicott's refreshing valuations.

The prominent themes of education and religion meld when Vida invites Carol to gain the town's trust by teaching Sunday school. As a one-time Congregationalist at a Universalist college still fighting the heresies of Voltaire, Darwin, and Ingersoll, agnostic Carol (who addresses God as "dear nebulous Lord") replies that her religion is foggy (36). (After a spell at Yale, Lewis found his own early devotion to Sunday school, Bible study, missions, and the muscular Christianity of the Young Men's Christian Association waning.) The important thing, pragmatic Vida counters, is belief in God, Jesus, and fellowship.

From another source, the savagely satirized Widow Bogart, Carol learns that the Baptist Church is superior to the Protestant Evangelical Church, for it has heeded the true principles of Christianity longer and better than any other church. Mrs. Bogart follows this up with the simpering hope that Carol Kennicott will declare for Will's own "vessel of faith" (72). Identifying faith with churchgoing, joyless Mrs. Bogart also hopes that Carol will keep the Sabbath. Until Carol loosens up her housewarming guests, she feels that her own Merry Mount has reached the decorum of the Sabbath. Playing Oriental princess to the hilt, Carol even converses with Guy Pollock on Chinese religion, about which, says the narrator, she knows nothing—thereby negating her youthful gleaning of Max Müller on Eastern religion.

If Judge Milford's teenage daughter has not read Müller too well—or for that matter, Balzac and Rabelais and Thoreau—we can believe that she at least had free reign of her father's library. Certainly the discordant attitudes in *Main Street* toward books, plays, magazines, newspapers, and film vivify the novel. A self-confessed bookworm, Carol reads "everything" (255), which, she believes, makes her "beastly oversensitive" (33). Indeed, her thoughts often are purely literary. Still, her willingness to differ from "book-ignoring" people is valiant (13). At Blodgett, where one "lady instructress" actually likes Milton and Carlyle (8), Carol appropriately meditates on in-vogue thesis-plays of Eugène Brieux and George Bernard Shaw. Her awakening to scientific town planning rests on her casual reading of a book on village improvements, which predisposes her to loathe slatternly Gopher Prairie.

As a schoolgirl she aspires to become a scholarly rather than merely a custodial librarian. Thus her frenzied reading as a St. Paul librarian is a mishmash—anthropology, the imagists, curry recipes, South Sea voyages, theosophy, real estate—the kind of reading Lewis himself engaged in as a young book reviewer in New York. Among Windy City Bohemians, Carol tunes in on chatter about Sigmund Freud, Romain Rolland, and other darlings of the avant-garde. To sell

Carol on married life in enlightened Gopher Prairie, Will, who knows next to nothing about literature, observes that Guy Pollock writes "regular" poetry (22). Carol is indeed impressed when Guy names for her his favorite authors: Sir Thomas Browne, Thoreau, Agnes Repplier, Arthur Symons, Claude Washburn, and Charles Flandrau. Especially appealing to Guy, one surmises, would be Browne's antiquarianism, Thoreau's withdrawals, and Repplier's grace. Symons is remembered today for *The Symbolist Movement in Literature* (1899), of lasting consequence to T. S. Eliot. Lewis here plugs a pair of Minnesota writers, friend and so-so novelist Washburn and the witty essayist Flandrau, whose *Harvard Episodes* (1897), a *succès de scandale,* young ivy-bound Lewis relished. For Vida Sherwin, however, literature must be utilitarian and inspirational. Unlike Carol, who defends honest observation, she expresses her reservations about Harold Frederic's cynicism in *The Damnation of Theron Ware* (1896), a background novel to *Main Street*'s village life and to *Elmer Gantry*'s ministerial.

But over and over, Carol learns that the world at large is indifferent or opposed to serious literature. On the train Will closets himself with a "saffron" detective story (28), not unlike the traveling Lewis himself, addicted not to the escapism of "historical" westerns or "futuristic" science fiction but rather to contemporary-costumed whodunits. Sam Clark's bookcase houses swashbuckler romances and unread sets of Dickens, Kipling, O. Henry, and Elbert Hubbard. Talkative Chet Dashaway asks Carol if she's read "Two Out" in *Tingling Tales.* Hustling Harry Haydock boasts, without a trace of irony, that his wife, Juanita, reads high-class stuff like *Mid the Magnolias* by Sara Hetwiggin Butts and *Riders of Ranch Reckless.*

Raymie Wutherspoon, defender of Henry Wadsworth Longfellow, holds with Vida Sherwin's view that literature should be pure and uplifting, stories wholesome and improving. Besides the "dandiest" reciters and minstrels (62), he appreciates motion pictures, because he can never be sure what's in a library book. Lewis augments his own prologual sarcasm about the "sensitive art" of the Rosebud Movie Palace being "strictly moral" (6) by having Raymie assert that at least a movie is censored. When Raymie crows that he had Balzac removed from the library—an author Carol had earlier read—a boardinghouse salesman asks where he can get a copy. In cities like St. Paul patrons go to the library for titillating love stories; in towns like Gopher Prairie they go to the library for Elsie books. For off-color magazines, they go to the tobacco shop.

Throughout *Main Street* the main character expresses interest not only in art but in sociology, political science, and economics. On the train to Gopher Prairie, Carol's glimpse of the ugliness of little Schoenstrom, hometown of flivver Galahad Milt Daggett in *Free Air,* prompts her to remark to Will that the wealth of its richest inhabitant—one wonders why not the second or third richest?—should go back into the settlement "where it belongs." The citizens there should burn the old shacks and build a dream-village. With more sound than fury, she asks, "Why do the farmers and the town-people let the Baron keep it?" (28). Unlike young "Red" Lewis, who worked at Helicon Hall—Upton Sinclair's socialistic community in Englewood, New Jersey—who preached socialism instead of Christianity at Yale, and who was a member of the Socialist party from January 1911 to April 1912, Carol thinks "socialist" in believing that farmers and workers should have more political power, the better to produce and distribute necessary goods. As the train moves northward, Carol, an advocate of social progress and scientific experimentation, wonders if this empty land will continue to harbor inequalities. Her wonder here is linked to the narrator's opening idea about the promise of the "bewildered empire."

Once in Gopher Prairie, Carol feels artistic contempt for raw commercialism and feminist contempt for old men who demand that women bear children. In another fanciful mood, Carol, perhaps recalling the man in shirtsleeves shaving the man with the large Adam's apple, asks Will, who hunts with his tailor, if he'd also hunt with his barber. Commonsensical Will sees "no use running this democracy thing into the ground" (45). Ezra Stowbody warns against immigrant farmers, Swedes especially, who instantly turn socialist or populist. Jackson Elder, who complains that labor trouble in his mill starts with mechanics reading anarchist books, regards complications, reports, wage scales, and profit sharing as "socialism in disguise" (53); welfare insurance and old-age pensions are poppycock, enfeeblers of independence and honest profit. Dave Dyer asserts, one assumes figuratively, that outside agitators should be hanged—and Will agrees. Although Will insists that farmers and townspeople are interdependent, Carol wonders if the latter are not parasites. While admitting to cranks in every class, Will opposes farmers running the state and fixing his fees. Ironically, Carol the "planner" has a budget book but no budget.

Planning might well be inventive, but following plans might well become routine—and Carol hates routine. One discerns in *Main Street* a rough equation between routine and standardization, between standardization and dullness, between dullness and blemish, between blemish and inertia, between inertia and death. Carol, in contrast, "could never be static" (9). So "alive" is she on her hilltop that though the deader-than-Camelot ghosts of the St. Paul's pioneer past surround her, she envisions only her immediate present and distant future. The standard faculty reception hints at the important death theme in *Main Street,* for the president's home is "massed with palms suggestive of polite undertaking parlors" (14). Even as a librarian, Carol feels shut off by the lifeless steel stacks and the inanimate stamped cards. On the dull trip to Gopher Prairie Carol watches the station agent hoisting a "dead calf aboard the baggage-car" (27). At the Gopher Prairie station she sees "unadventurous people with dead eyes" (31). A marble slab in the Kennicott bedroom looks like a "gravestone"; the judgmental furniture condemns Carol to death by smothering. In short, the old house "smelled of the tomb" (35).

Among these Poe-like shadows of dead thoughts and haunting repressions, Carol feels isolated. As she walks down homely Main Street, she sees a distant windmill—symbolic perhaps of her future tilting—that resembles the ribs of a "dead cow" (37). From the meat market, she smells the reek of blood; in a clothing-store window she sees suits "flabbily draped on dummies like corpses with painted cheeks" (39). Then, too, the various sets at the Clarks' party "sat up with gaiety as with a corpse" (49). Finally, squeamish Carol is reluctant to shake hands with wide-mouthed Chet Dashaway, furniture dealer and embalmer. Out on the restorative prairie, however, the three prairie chickens that Will shoots give to his fastidious young wife no sensation of blood, no hint of death.

Indeed, as at first Carol looked upon the small town as an escape from her city job, so by the end of the first section she looks upon the open country as an escape from the small town. So glaring is the escape motif in *Main Street* that one might well think of the novel as a modern captivity narrative. Carol's impulse to flee painful realities sets the tone. In the novel's opening scene, Lewis has her "fleeing for an hour" from Blodgett ivy (7). Her dipping later into a supplementary text on village improvements is, like much of her reading, largely escapism, for she "had fled half-way through it" before the start of her dull history class (11). As she flies from Stewart Snyder's ardor, so a month after graduation she foregoes writing to him. Though here Carol is strong and energetic enough to break away from Stewart's picture of marital bliss in Yankton, later in St. Paul she is too weary from library work and too weakened by Will's resolution to evade the promise of his fuzzy photos.

On her Colorado honeymoon, Carol finds passion and release, but on the trip to Gopher Prairie she wonders if she has bound herself to Will and his town "inescapably" (30). That she *will* find life there unendurable—clearly foreshadowed in this scene—becomes self-fulfilling prophecy. Marriage means forcible restraint: "She would have to wrench loose from this man and flee" (31). She envisions flight toward the Pacific. Still preoccupied with liberation, she views Will's drop-in at his office as an escape to "the world of men's affairs" (35). More important, she suddenly conceives of childbearing as entrapment. Only her fear of the encroaching prairie drives her back to the musty Kennicott house after her maiden stroll down Main Street. In the custody of bores at the Clarks' party, Carol surmises that the guests' impatience for food comes from their hunger for distraction, for release from their inglorious selves.

The rebellious college girl envisioning her future from her hilltop does indeed expect some sort of glory for herself. Until Will comes along she foresees no man to serve, and even after she marries Will she rejects the idea of his defining her future. She wonders about the prospects for the northern Midwest, but Will predicts a great future.

With automobiles, telephones, and mail delivery, future farmers will be open to larger experiences and their children will prosper. Hamlets like Schoenstrom will match the comfort of small towns like Gopher Prairie. But nothing in the railroad settlements will change, Carol believes, if left to chance. Although Vida Sherwin assures Carol that the spirit of Gopher Prairie is sound and that the town will change for the better, Carol sees its spirit as dark and unconquerable.

5

Carol D'Arc

As benighted as Gopher Prairie might be to Carol Kennicott, she strives nevertheless in the next six chapters (7 through 12) to lead her husband and her town upward toward her vision of goodness, truth, and beauty. Unfortunately, she meets with failure after failure—in upgrading taste, promoting winter sport, gossiping with the bridge set, discussing Will's practice, reading Will poetry, enriching the women's study club, erecting a new city hall, uplifting the poor, forming a salon, and surveying local history.

More particularly, Carol fails in chapter 7 to persuade her friends to repeat parties of skating, sledding, and skiing. Feeling lonely and spied upon, she decides to become a Nice Married Woman, but quarrels with members of Gopher Prairie's "social cornice" (88), the Jolly Seventeen, over servants' wages and book preservation. She endeavors to query Will about his cases in chapter 8, but his mind is on supper and the furnace. On the painful day that Vida Sherwin tells Carol that folks see her as "showing off" (96), Lewis convincingly has Will tell her to trade more with his patients and buy more from Gopher Prairie shops than from Twin Cities stores.

In chapter 9 we see Carol avoiding people. Detesting the amicable rudeness of Yankee merchants, she shops with the Scandinavian farmwives at Axel Egge's. Leered at by the street-corner roués, she later overhears two, Cyrus Bogart and Earl Haydock, discoursing on her anatomy and undergarments. Renewed doubts about her marriage dissolve after she visits her mother-in-law in Lac-qui-Meurt. This improvisational visit to the Big Woods ("She had her first sight of Will's mother, except the glimpse at the wedding") is as unconvincing as her *not* visiting Will's mother in Gopher Prairie before the wedding (106). Lewis signals his heroine's alienation by making Bea Sorenson, Carol's hired girl, her best friend. Still, when Will is out of town with a patient the doctor's wife feels lonely.

Though in chapter 10 versatile Carol Kennicott effervesces again, Lewis relentlessly exhibits the difficulty of changing Gopher Prairie. Carol even fails, albeit good-naturedly, to plant the seed of poetry in her own home. Craving company, a more diplomatic Carol rejoins the Jolly Seventeen. Her own poor bridge playing embarrasses her less than hearing the young matrons exposing their husbands' habits. When the Thanatopsis Club invites Carol to comment on today's topic—"English Poetry"—she sees it as an opportunity to "liberalize" Philistia (124). Inspired by a casual remark from this pathetic, this laughable, group (a far cry from Zona Gale's delight in her "Friendship Village Married Ladies' Cemetery Improvement Sodality"), Carol (ludicrously ingenuous herself) dreams up a new "city hall" (127). But her Georgian fantasies, based largely on pictures in library magazines, are dashed—first by Mrs. Warren (wife of the Congregational minister), next by Mrs. Mott (wife of the school superintendent), and then by Mrs. Dyer (the druggist's wife).

Into her expandable dream edifice Carol nobly incorporates courtroom, library, prints, restroom, kitchen, theater, ballroom, farm bureau, domestic science demonstrations, lecture halls, gymnasium, a farmwives' clubroom, and even a school, but the people of Gopher Prairie see no need for new buildings and new taxes. When Carol naively invites tight-fisted Luke Dawson to begin rebuilding the town, the milky-faced millionaire informs her that he and his wife plan to move to a bungalow in California.

Unable to assent to Miles Bjornstam's cynical if not bloody proposition that someday the "cheerful bums" will simply take things away from the Dawsons of the world (139), Carol suggests that the Thanatopsis teach the poor self-help, but even this the club checkmates. Chapter 12 points up Carol's lackluster life when, on one of her solitary spring walks to the outskirts of town, she again runs into Bjornstam, just starting off with his friend Pete Rustad for a summer of horsetrading in the Rockies. Still, Carol's own summer of swimming, picnicking, and gossiping at the cottage on Lake Minniemashie brings contentment not felt in the house on Poplar Street.

In the fall the Kennicotts celebrate their first anniversary with Vida and Guy, but Carol's dream of a salon flops. Turning to local history, she interviews the Champ Perrys, only to discover in their pioneer simplicity a reactionary narrow-mindedness. In the last terse episode of this second set of six chapters, a smiling Carol greets a jubilant Miles Bjornstam, just back from Montana. Though Carol Kennicott and her handyman friend are by no means forerunners of D. H. Lawrence's Lady Chatterley and her gamekeeper lover, Lewis's little cliff-hanging collocation here does tease the imagination.

Less suggestive is Lewis's intrusive narrator, who in this section comments on problems—of economics, of status, of marriage—endemic to the larger world. The wrangling in Jolly Seventeen over how much to pay a hired girl echoes global conflicts: international orators are "but the raised voices of a billion Juanitas denouncing a million Carols, with a hundred thousand Vida Sherwins trying to shoo away the storm" (92). Prosperous Yankee merchants, the narrator later persists, are unconsciously rude to the doctor's wife out of egalitarian principles, and "Old Country" storekeepers are gruff because they want to be taken for prosperous Yankee merchants. Finally, the insightful narrator comments on wives who, like Carol, eternally ask if their marriages are a mistake.

Though Carol is not altogether immune to the author's lively satire, Lewis hurls nearly all of his barbs in this section at Main Street's deep-rooted aversion to change; at its women's clubs, shallow culture, and juvenile delinquency; at its opposition to civic spending, to women in politics, and to the poor; at its living in the past. Still, there is radical technological change, which enables pompous auto-owning villagers to look upon activities like skiing and sliding as "old-fashioned" (84). Bridge also enfeebles physical activity and underscores the town's social divisions. Lewis satirizes the Jolly Seventeen as killing time by cardplaying, gossiping, and wolfing "refreshments" (90). Lewis pokes fun at the Haydocks' varnished and the Dawsons' faded tastes. Laughable also are the Thanatopsis women who read one another disjointed facts copied out of encyclopedias. Carol, too, cuts a ridiculous figure as she muses on her all-encompassing city hall as a fait accompli. Lewis mocks Thanatopsis members for not depriving themselves the pleasure of bestowing charity and insults on the poor. Again, Lewis smiles at Carol for naively trying to turn back the clock by taking up the Champ Perrys' Old West.

Lewis's joy in cataloging Gopher Prairie—listings often implicitly satirical—is obvious. In describing the town "digging in for the winter" (82), the narrator itemizes the kind of garments ("armor") that the villagers dig out of their closets and drawers (84). That sure sign of winter, handyman Miles Bjornstam, has accoutrements that Lewis joyfully names. As he ticks off the intimacies of the Jolly Seventeen, so he enumerates the gossip of the Thanatopsis. The register of the pretentious furniture in the Haydock concrete bungalow and the record of the useless objects that look like other objects in the "crammed Victorian school" of the Cass parlor (135) highlight the inventories of hodgepodge in Axel Egge's Scandinavian store, the farmwives' restroom, and the Perry rooms above Howland & Gould's Grocery. Alongside Lewis's roll call of busy village industries is his contrasting string of miserable outskirt sights.

Twice in this section problem-ridden Carol searches her memory for a usable past. In the first instance, a weeping Carol, having learned that Gopher Prairie regards her as a show-off, seeks comfort not in her husband but in her father, "her smiling understanding father, dead these twelve years" (98). In the second instance, Carol is perplexed by her preference for the companionship not of Jolly Seventeen matrons but of her spontaneous and unpedigreed hired girl. However sympathetic to the lower half, Carol "had been reared to assume that servants belong to a distinct and inferior species" (108). In both instances, Carol's personal past fails her.

Even the outcome of those wonderful "dressing-up" parties seems in vain. In her tam o'shanter, loose nutria coat, and tweed skirt, Carol feels as happy as a hooky-playing schoolgirl, only to learn from Vida that some Gopher Prairieites think she dresses too well. As always, Lewis has Carol jumping to extremes, when she suggests that her wearing a gunny sack might suit them. To increase Carol's self-consciousness about her new checked suit even further, Lewis has her overhear Cy Bogart apprising Earl Haydock not only of her low-cut dresses in public but of her "shimmy shirts" on the clothesline (105). If some think Carol dresses too well, Carol's maid at least is appreciative. While Bea, in her blue gingham apron, lunches in the kitchen, Carol, in her gold-edged black satin frock, lunches in the dining room. For her enterprising library visit, Carol dons her sober blue suit and organdy collar.

Of her face and figure in this section, Lewis tells us only that her hair (admired by Bea) is "elegant" (108) and that her cheeks (unlined by village jealousies) are "virginal" (113). Ankle-conscious Cy Bogart calls her a "good-looker" (105), but after Carol overhears his chatter about Will's premarital "chewing," she confesses to herself that for all her superiority she, too, partakes in human filth, eats and digests, washes her "dirty paws" and scratches. "I'm not a cool slim goddess on a column. There aren't any" (106).

Still, ungodly Carol, later tittering at a lowbrow Rosebud movie, "mourned for the day when on her hill by the Mississippi she had walked the battlements with queens" (121). Earlier than this poignant scene, she wonders if her "real level" is kitchen gossip with Bea (112). To be sure, on her dreary winter hillside Carol feels much too cold to look down on Gopher Prairie with any superiority. But the idealism/height motif reappears in the spring when Carol, on a country walk, turns for an enchanted hour "to youth and a belief in the possibility of beauty" (143); Miles, who views Carol as a silver gull flying over dirty seals, facetiously invites her to join him and Pete Rustad on their horsetrading ramble high up in the Big Horn Mountains. Though the Kennicotts' Minniemashie cottage is not on a mountaintop, it is, at least, on a bluff.

And though high-minded Carol is deeply wounded by Gopher Prairie's mean-minded feelings toward her, she can still sympathize and want to belong. Will is hard to mother, but Carol can still relate to friendly women and to women who toil. To the irritation of the Jolly Seventeen, however, she defends paying Bea more than the others pay their maids. At Thanatopsis, Carol's heart goes out to little Mrs. Hicks, so awed by the group; and so considerate is Mrs. Perry that Carol suddenly feels affection for the club's pathetic cultural efforts. And, of course, Carol includes in her chimerical city hall a new restroom for the farmwives. When this figment evaporates, she fancies once more doing something for the impoverished, though now she refers to the poor as the "unpicturesque" (140), not, as at Blodgett, the "grateful" (11).

In fact, as the novelty of romanticizing aspects of Gopher Prairie wears off, Carol turns more and more to her world of fantasy. At first, tramping happily uptown in the fresh snow, she looks upon a can of tomatoes as Oriental fruit and dreams up a surprise dinner for Will. When the snow is no longer fresh, however, she loses her enthusiasm for town, people, and sports. Still, she finds Axel Egge's store "so picturesque and romantic" (102). In truth, Main Street's limited meats—steaks, pork, ham—are sufficient material to tax anyone's culinary ingenuity.

In agreeing to birth control, Carol wonders if Will "had made all the mystery of love a mechanical cautiousness" (86). She fancies that she would prefer secretly to learn that her husband, before marriage, had a vice worthier than tobacco-chewing—gambling or keeping a mistress. On one of Will's absences she pretends that she is entertaining clever men. She imagines tropical mists, Paris nights, Baghdad walls. Closer to home, she imagines reading poetry with Will over large fair pages next to an imaginary fireplace. One lonely night she imagines that the house is haunted. In one of her walks she passes a mill and wishes that she could work there, not be simply a professional man's wife. Miles buoys up her imagination. She reads Yeats and is transported to his poetic world. So suppositious is Carol that she believes her campaign against village sloth actually has begun.

Daydreaming in the public library, Carol adroitly pictures a more pleasant reading room, chairs for children, an art collection, a librarian young enough to experiment. She broods over magazine pictures of quaint places not in the Midwest. In imagination she raises her splendid city hall. Immune to the reality of historical continuity, she modifies her dream hall as she feels the deep-rooted resistance to "science" or "progress." The stupid town cannot keep her, at any rate, from loving her foolish dream of Venice. In the end, Carol decides that "Her home, and her beautiful town, existed in her mind" (138). The task was done. Her true great quest is for a never-to-be-found someone to share her "creation"—some spirit in Gopher Prairie as young and unreasonable as hers. She moves from dreams of a new prairie architecture to dreams of a new way to help the poor to dreams of a simpler, sturdier, heroic past. But after one evening of hearing the reactionary Perrys hold forth, her conventional piety toward old pioneers suddenly vanishes.

However dreamy Carol might be, she clearly is at times Sinclair Lewis's sociological mouthpiece, as when she blurts out at Jolly Seventeen, "How much do maids get here?" (91). Generalizing from her friendly relations with Bea, Carol argues that employers might well contribute to the ungratefulness of maids by granting them only leftovers. As an isolato following the dispute, Carol is under the illusion that she is thinking more sharply than she has been thinking for weeks. She idealistically suggests that Thanatopsis take up chemistry, anthropology, and—perhaps thinking of Miles's opinions—labor problems. But so emotional is Carol that she finds it difficult to be "impersonal" (96).

As for physical exaltation in this second part, Carol's fingertips love the silken nutria fur. She so loves the first snowfall that on her radiant return home from shopping she runs, leaps, and shouts like a schoolgirl until, feeling eyes on her, she self-consciously assumes the role of Mrs. Dr. Kennicott. Even though the novelty of snow wears off, Carol suggests another bobsled party, but the Jolly Seventeen shows no enthusiasm. She revels in her visit to Lac-qui-Meurt. Later she tramps in 30-below weather but feels too cold for exhilaration. In May she walks to Plover Lake and once again joys in nature, in freedom after winter's grip. Escaping Gopher Prairie, she contents herself with outdoor activities at Lake Minniemashie.

Introspective Carol spends much time wondering if Gopher Prairie likes her. Doubts prompt her defensive outpourings and whimsies. She blames her touchiness for the Jolly Seventeen fiasco, but she seems unaware of any self-pity in pronouncing herself an outcast to Vida. Carol speaks truth when she explains that she might be "affected and culturine," but not so vulgar as to pretend that Will is richer than he is. From thinking that no one is staring at her, Carol tells herself that everyone is staring—that she is preposterous, paranoic, to be so sensitive. After acknowledging village curiosity as a reality, Carol, as usual, rebounds. She asks herself if she wants something to mother—a man, a baby, a town—and if she had found her social and intellectual level in Bea.

Early in this section Carol realizes that she is "a woman with a working brain and no work" (86). That she feels suddenly unmarried, thinks freely of Guy Pollock, plays the piano, and sings is psychologically convincing. She admonishes herself for patronizing the Thanatopsis: "Stop this fever of reforming everything!" (128). Like the author, Carol finds dishonesty and stupidity in all human activity. The quaint magazine villages assure her, however, that she is "not quite mad" (130). But after a string of rebukes, Carol sees herself as a fool. "I dream of Venice, and I live in Archangel and scold because the Northern seas aren't tender-colored" (137). How, she wonders, had she fallen into the folly of trying to plant aesthetic seeds in Gopher Prairie? But in alignment with the character that he has created, Lewis makes Carol soon dream of planting communalistic seeds, though even this latest inspiration she does not consciously trace to its immediate source—her little exchange on Main Street with Miles Bjornstam.

Again, when not tasting the fatness and flavor of praise, Carol begins to doubt herself. Self-doubt makes her oversensitive to nuance and gesture, putting her, therefore, in the uncustomary position of a wallflower. Only sexy Rita Simon's genuine admiration for Carol's steel-buckled shoes brings a modicum of relief. So low is Carol's threshold of social pain that she is even relieved to overhear lascivious Cy telling Earl that she is "all right, I guess" (105). Heartened by sundry welcomes home after the Lac-qui-Meurt visit, Carol yet must convince herself, delicately and irrelevantly, that she prefers "violins in a paneled room" to "shouts on Main Street" (107).

More honest is her perceiving Bea's adulation for her as "the admiration of Freshman for Junior" (108). However uncomfortable Carol might feel as comrade to "a pipe-reeking odd-job man" (114), she asks Miles a loaded question: Would *he* worry if people thought *him* affected? The nonconformist handyman's "kick'em in the face!" emboldens the doctor's wife (118); but instead of taking his advice, Carol longs to be part of Jolly Seventeen, daughter to the Thanatopsis, one of the "young folks" who take the pioneering Perrys seriously. Lewis has her go so far as to pretend that the group is right about maids' wages, that she wants the recipe for the divine angel food cake, and that, although her own refreshments are inferior, she aspires to entertain the group.

Carol's desire for acceptance (if not for admiration) and the pressures of conformity shape her social hypocrisy. While twittering apologies for her inability to play bridge, Carol snarls to herself: "That ought to be saccharine enough" (89). For sarcastic Mrs. Howland she also wears a false face: "I think that is the prettiest display of beef-tea your husband has in his store" (89). Carol inquires about Mrs. McGanum's baby and even smiles in agreement with Miss Villets's library views. But her hypocrisy has not saved her from the wolves.

Ironically, she asks Vida if she, Carol, must find dishonesty and stupidity everywhere. When she cannot evade certain people, she talks trivia. "Always she was acting . . . for the benefit of the ambushed leering eyes which she did not see" (100). Desiring to get into Miss Villets's good graces, she "lied resolutely" about how sorry she was not to see her at Thanatopsis (128). As the whimpering Villets fishes for compliments, Carol obliges, applying her little white lies with a trowel. Even to Mrs. Perry she forswears herself, declaring that Gopher Prairie "had the color of Algiers and the gaiety of Mardi Gras" (135).

Color and gaiety are, of course, precisely what Carol sees Gopher Prairie as lacking. From her dreary hilltop vantage, Carol sees the town wiped out by snow. The reader is as surprised as Carol to learn that Gopher Prairie is legally a city, with a mayor and a city council—and that it likes to think of itself as such. Still, to Carol's dismay, people do not share her idealism, do not want to tear down and rebuild; they like their trees, lawns, comfortable houses, hot water, electricity, telephones, and paved walks. Not in 20 years, Will tells his wife, would the council and the citizens vote funds for a new city hall. The harsh town of rain and snow that Lewis portrays—reminding one at times of Edith Wharton's Starkfield, Massachusetts, in *Ethan Frome* (1911)—enables Carol to tell herself that this "morass" is not her home (138). Again, although Lewis does not describe Main Street itself in this section, we see Carol there, know what she is seeing and feeling, and understand why she needs a room of her own.

While she is proud of her Japanesque decor in the living room, others regard her couch and obi as absurd. Still, she naively believes that her charming example can uplift Gopher Prairie interiors. But when Carol overhears flowing down from her own garage loft Cyrus's blab to Earl, she feels she has been "dragged naked down Main Street" (105). Even after lowering her shades at dusk, she still feels "moist fleering eyes" (106). Carol's loneliness, her fear, her husband's absence, and finally her fleeing from the hollow "creepy" house (112) bring to mind the prairie gothicism that permeates E. W. Howe's *The Story of a Country Town* (1883).

Although the prairie inhabitants are cordial, they are on the watch, testing every newcomer. They express to Carol the same enjoyment of her outdoor events that they expressed about her housewarming, but they do not emulate them. For Eastern Star and Fireman's Ball dances to rival each other is in Gopher Prairie good form. It is also good form for the customers to bicker good-naturedly with merchants, a sport the aristocratical Carol detests.

She also finds her first encounter with the Jolly Seventeen odious. The occasion offers Lewis the opportunity to reveal the clique's gratifications, vulgarity, and smugness. Between 14 and 26 mostly young married women play bridge weekly, hold a bridge-and-supper monthly, and sponsor select dances twice yearly. At the weekly afternoon affairs they devour the standard coffee, rolls, olives, potato salad, and cake. After her fiasco with the group, Carol attends only the monthly suppers with Will; but having renewed her courage by learning elemental bridge at the Clarks', Carol attends the weekly bridge at Maud Dyer's. Playing quietly and "reasonably bad" (121), Carol is dismayed by the women's bad taste in exposing their domestic intimacies. When, to ingratiate herself, Carol expresses a desire to host a weekly bridge, Juanita suggests something cunning and original but not too queer or freaky. Jolly Seventeen is, after all, "a pretty good bunch"—its collective brow might be lower than Minneapolis or St. Paul's, but it is higher than Wakamin or Joralemon's (122).

Between the Jolly Seventeen and the Thanatopsis is some overlap, though the "in" group looks down on the women's study group as middle-class and intellectual. (For many years Lewis's stepmother, Isabel Warner, served Sauk Centre's Gradatim Club [which had the motto, "Heaven is not reached at a single bound"], the real counterpart of Thanatopsis.) Vida, behind everything, invites Carol to the club, known for its stimulating papers, civic activities, and up-to-date ideas. Dubious Carol wonders if she might not use the club for her crusade to liberalize the town. Indeed, throughout America at the time women banded together to better living conditions with sanitation, tree planting, nurseries, censorship, and beautification. After failure, Carol's attitude is: "What do I care for Thanatopsises?" (144). Without intending to, she eventually neglects her tasks in connection with the club's salutary anti-fly campaign.

Thus, Carol's place as Gopher Prairie's liberalizing role model becomes increasingly problematic. Even before the newcomer's pretentious crusading, Vida had pointed up the town's attitude toward Carol's affectations by alluding to the broad *A* of a former Latin teacher from Wellesley College. Too quick to react to Mrs. Mott's hint that the town needs a new school building, Carol investigates the old damp yellow school and ascertains that its jail-like windows express hate and compulsion. With little thought, she incorporates a school into her vision of a city hall. But not all the townspeople, Carol learns, support education. Mrs. Perry, for example, informs Carol that a sermon is better than a lecture, that the town is full of geography books and things nobody needs to know, and that even at Thanatopsis one finds heathen learning. Lewis pokes fun at bogus education when he has Carol learn that Lyman Cass's son has graduated from Chicopee Falls Business College, McGillicuddy University. In a show of proletarian bravado, Miles confides that when they get educated the "cheerful bums" will take over (139).

Even this swagger Carol finds preferable to Gopher Prairie's sanctimoniousness. She resents suggestions from various quarters that she attend church more. She cannot abide the Gopher Prairie God who speaks in doggerel hymns, those mocked by Lewis, most often with tongue in cheek. Even Thanatopsis is churchly, interested less in literary art than in moral instruction. As Mrs. Dawson phrases it, poets provide "inspiration for higher thought" (124). Rather than a new city hall, Mrs. Warren prefers an all-evangelical clubhouse. Besides remarking on the sinful paganism of the Russian church—no doubt meaning the militant atheism of the Communist party—she proclaims that the chief ornament of the Christian church is charity, the pleasure of giving to the "grateful" poor (140), Carol's own patronizing modifier back at Blodgett. But nothing could harm the poor if they took up Christian Science, declares Mrs. Mary Ellen Wilks, her name a parody of Christian Science founder Mary Baker Eddy. Feeling that there is enough of Mrs. Warren's "Grand Old Book" in church and Sunday school (142), Carol balks at more Bible study in Thanatopsis. A little later the fundamentalist Champ Perrys heavy-handedly inform Carol of the need to get back to the word of God and a belief in hell, back to the perfect Baptist standard. Meanwhile, Carol feels happiest in the pagan outdoors: "I believe! The woodland gods still live!" (144).

For all her passion, particularly her literary passion, Carol is devoid of creative literary talent. Mercifully, Lewis at least has his critical Carol recognize the poetic ineptitude of her "The sky is bright, the sun is warm, there n'er will be another storm" (85). Later, in *Cass Timberlane,* Lewis has poetaster Dr. Allan Cedar indite analogous atmospherical banality: "It is snowing, The wind is blowing, But I am happy to be going."[11] Appropriately enough, it is through wearisome escapist magazine love stories that Carol makes her sudden discovery about having "nothing to do" (86).

Later she pushes aside the *Saturday Evening Post,* the *Literary Digest, National Geographic,* and Joseph Conrad. If the Conrad characterizes Carol's respect for serious literature, the *Saturday Evening Post* reveals Carol as not unwilling to read—as Lewis was not unwilling to write for—George Horace Lorimer's mass-appeal magazine. The high-circulation *Literary Digest* would expose Carol (and owlish Julius Flickerbaugh) to weekly condensations of current thought. Unlike Conrad's recondite word painting, *National Geographic* prose is negligible, but its brilliant photography, its images of faraway places with strange-sounding names, still brings solace to armchair vagabonds like Carol.

That Carol the bookworm and former librarian has not visited, let alone patronized, the town library before now seems dubious. At any rate, Lewis contrives to have Miss Villets boast at the Jolly Seventeen that Gopher Prairie has 2,000 more books than Wakamin. Unsympathetic to Carol's tolerance for "poor souls" who loiter in city libraries (93), Miss Villets also declares that a librarian's chief task is to preserve books. Carol's non sequitur about books being cheaper than minds prompts Miss Villets's non sequitur about the library as no nursing home or kindergarten. Assuaged later by Carol's first visit to the library and by her flattery, Miss Villets escorts her to the old-magazine files where she muses on the photographs. When her thick-coming architectural fancies do not materialize, Carol mulls over records of the *Minnesota Territorial Pioneers* instead.

Deploring the absence of literary sensitivity in most American men, Carol gathers from fiction that in this country only the virile can function. Still, she wishes that Will (with whose premarital tobacco-chewing she cannot identify) were as literate as "book-drugged" Guy (120). Her success in singing Scottish ballads to Will one evening encourages Carol to try poetry on him. No sooner does she begin reading Yeats than she is transported to the mythical old Gaelic world—only to be interrupted by Will's coughing. Responsive to the spirit of her uphill enterprise, however, he bravely alludes to that homespun verser James Whitcomb Riley and to Henry Wadsworth Longfellow's "The Song of Hiawatha," famous in Minnesota more for Minnehaha Falls than for trochaic tetrameter. Carol next tries the dulcet tapestry of Tennyson's *Idylls of the King,* metrical romances that awed Lewis as a Sauk Centre boy. Finally, unable to experience Camelot, Carol declaims Rudyard Kipling, that idol of adventurous youngsters since the 1890s, and Will even joins in. Still, they end up at the Rosebud Movie Palace. Failing to spread sweetness and light, Carol is nevertheless relieved to discover that by summertime she no longer pines for bookish conversation.

When Carol finally agrees to brighten a Thanatopsis meeting, she is delighted by the housewives' interest in poetry, but she is disheartened by the inclusiveness of today's topic: English poetry. She listens to dreary, self-satisfied biographies of "Shakespeare and Milton," "Byron, Scott, Moore, and Burns," "Tennyson and Browning," and "Other Poets." She listens to Ella Stowbody recite old chestnuts like "The Recessional," extracts from *Lalla Rookh,* and, as an encore, "An Old Sweetheart of Mine." When Carol diplomatically suggests that the women next take up the topic in more detail, especially the poetry of Keats, Arnold, Rossetti, and Swinburne, Mrs. Warren takes exception to what she understands is the absence in Swinburne of heartfelt message. Still, the club votes for some future meeting devoted "entirely" to English poetry (127). Coffee and cake, quips the narrator, help the members recover from the depression of Shakespeare's death. At the meeting devoted to "English Fiction and Essays," Carol listens to statistics on Dickens, Thackeray, Austen, George Eliot, Scott, Hardy, Lamb, De Quincey, and—in typical Lewisian anticlimax—Mrs. Humphrey Ward. At the next meeting, the club takes up, more absurdly, the literature of Scandinavia, Russia, and Poland. Poor Carol can only praise Mrs. Westlake's lucubration on Tolstoy.

Other readers in this section range from Miles Bjornstam to a "small flaxen boy" (129). Miles's books are as incongruous as Guy's. Manuals on gas engines and farm animals share a shelf with romantics Byron, Tennyson, Stevenson, and the satiric social diagnostician Thorstein Veblen, famous for his *Theory of the Leisure Class* (1899). The flaxen boy withdrawing *Frank on the Lower Mississippi* from the library seems like an old memory of Sinclair Lewis himself borrowing a book from Sauk Centre's Bryant Library. Vital winter reading for Jolly Seventeeners is the bridge manual. Behind his hand the narrator laughs at the illustrated gift edition on Juanita Haydock's table; the poetic motto and the photograph of the Falls of Minnehaha in the Lyman Cass parlor; and Champ Perry's observation that Harold Bell Wright is a lovely writer because his novels teach "good morals"—and "folks say he's made prett' near a million dollars out of 'em" (151). The unjust relationship between deficient literary talent and excessive monetary reward was always a sore point with Lewis.

He makes Carol, like himself in the 1910s, believe in a more equitable distribution of national income. And also, like himself, he makes her speak out for liberals, labor unions, socialists, and suffragists. After she learns that the Jolly Seventeen looks upon her paying Bea $6 a week as dangerous competition, she also decides that Gopher Prairie is devoid of industrial justice. Obviously, Lewis's exposé of the slum shacks of Swede Hollow, his largely sympathetic treatment of Scandinavian immigrants, and his allusion to the "wise chatterers" of Stockholm (113) did him no harm in his successful bid for the Nobel Prize in 1930. Carol would like to do something for the citizens of Swede Hollow, but she also feels that they would resent her playing Lady Bountiful. Miles reveals to her his friendly arguments with a dogmatic old-line closet socialist, Lyman Cass's foreman. More radical than his friend, the Red Swede believes that the ship of state is too far gone for reform—it must be rebuilt. He is amused by Carol's surprise to learn from him about a proletarian philosophy. But the reader is even more surprised, for one has assumed from the beginning—given Carol's college sociology, readings in economics and politics, comments to Will, and questions to the solid citizens—that she has, if not a sophisticated, at least a rudimentary knowledge of Marxism.

Unlike Carol, old-timers like the Perrys see no need for farm bureaus, domestic-science demonstrations, and scientific farming. The mill owner's wife, interested less in Tolstoy's art than in his politics, compliments Mrs. Dr. Westlake for pointing out in the Thanatopsis paper how all the author's "silly socialistic ideas failed" (136). Vida, who refers to Carol as the Joan of Arc of the hired girls, further cautions: "You mention the word 'co-operative' to the merchants and they'll lynch you!" (137). Finally, the Thanatopsis declines Carol's invitation to reflect on labor problems. Over such problems Sinclair Lewis himself brooded for many years as he planned and researched but never wrote a "labor novel."

Lewis's images of death in this section remain as paradoxically alive as in the first section. Carol's long cry after the Jolly Seventeen imbroglio occurs in the "shuttered and airless" black-walnut guestroom (94). When she inquires about Will's cases, he mentions "a fool woman that thinks she wants to kill herself because her husband doesn't like her" (94). Not only do the village lambs not like her, conjectures Carol, but they are wolves with "fangs and sneering eyes" (100). The snow turns gray and the trees black. The icy roads are gashed with ruts and houses look like specks on a white sheet. Swede Hollow harbors "misery and dead hope" (113). Near the slaughterhouse Carol sees "blood-marks on the snow" (114). In a tombstone-yard a whistling sculptor hammers on a shiny granite headstone. Carol learns of a poor town mother with 10 children, their father killed by a passing train. As earlier the imaginary queen of her youth fled into the darkness, so at the end of this section her images of stalwart pioneers fade like "daguerreotypes in a black walnut cupboard" (151).

This section is not without its flights and evasions. Dashing home after her exchange with the Jolly Seventeen, Carol cries: "And these women are to be my arbiters, the rest of my life!" (94). When she spots two members on Main Street, "She wanted to flee"—envisaging asylum in big-city indifference (100). Again, when she overhears Cyrus and Earl's garage talk, "Carol fled" (105). After two amiable days of escape to Lac-qui-Meurt, Carol returns to Gopher Prairie, but on the second day of Will's absence she again shuns the old house. Running back from her freezing hillside, she protests that she wants no drab in-between village; she wants either the sophisticated city or the primitive country. Even at her first Thanatopsis meeting, the insecure Carol feels like running. She later confides to Vida: "And sometime I'll run away—All right. No more" (137). But the fine May day she tramps into the countryside undercuts her resolve. Still, at Miles's flirtatious invitation to trek into the Rockies, Carol laughs: "Perhaps someday I'll do it" (146). Meanwhile, for a week at Lac-qui-Meurt and for the summer at Lake Minniemashie she finds temporary escape from Main Street.

With the future stretching before her, Carol as a doctor's wife in Gopher Prairie sees three possibilities: children, reform, activities. Since neither she nor Will is ready for the first, she vows to direct at Main Street her impulses toward beauty; as for activities, she considers church, study club, and bridge. Thwarted by the Jolly Seventeen, however, she is no longer sure that her ambition is to make this smug town better. She knows that she wants everything from being tolerated to a mahogany tea table. But rather than admit defeat, a lonely, sobbing Carol reverts to her resolution to reform the town, believing that the meek, the wolf-eaten, shall not inherit the earth.

Since Carol cannot accept Gopher Prairie's fears, prejudice, and intellectual squalor, she self-righteously believes that, for sheer survival, she *must* make it take her point of view. At one point, the malcontented housewife comes to believe that if only Will were as literate as Guy and Guy as vigorous as Will, she could endure even Gopher Prairie. "She needed a spirit as young and unreasonable as her own" (138). But believing also that she never will find this spirit, she turns simplistically to the past, to local history: "If she could not have ballrooms of gray and rose and crystal, she wanted to be swinging across a puncheon-floor with a dancing fiddler" (149).

6

Lady Bountiful

Showing us a Carol who despises Gopher Prairie's smug "in-between," its lack both of old heroism and new sophistication, Lewis in part 3 (chapters 13 through 18) reveals Carol's noblesse-oblige trials, first as medical helpmate and then as drama director. In chapter 13, a single scene, Guy Pollock expounds his village virus theory and confesses his loss of ambition. In the next chapter, also atypically unepisodic, Carol resolves not to fall in love with Guy, even after she and Will have their first serious quarrel.

This leads, in chapter 15, to Carol's romanticizing her role as doctor's wife and Will as doctor-hero. Her call on gossipy Mrs. Bogart makes her even happier to return to Will, who takes for granted the vicissitudes of country surgery and prairie blizzards. On Christmas Day, however, Carol, in chapter 16, weeps for yuletides past. Lewis follows this scene with information about Will's hobbies, American films, and another falling-out between the Kennicotts. Struggling to "go on" (200), to "grow" (199), to "save my soul" (196), Carol now perceives Guy as not so much enigmatical as faint-hearted. Meanwhile, Miles Bjornstam woos Bea Sorenson. Chapter 17 skillfully treats Carol's dubious formation of the Gopher Prairie Dramatic Association and the Kennicotts' play watching in Minneapolis. Instead of Carol's choice of Shaw's *Androcles and the Lion,* the selection committee in chapter 18 votes to put on a popular Broadway play. The production is a fiasco, but the *Dauntless* nevertheless hails the event as a triumph. In its wake, Carol, withering on the village vine, longs for escape.

The omniscient author, less conspicuous here than in the first two sections, expatiates on Carol's self-expression in the office of understanding Guy and on her self-pity in the office of unperceiving Will. Of Will's hobbies—medicine, land investment, Carol, motoring, hunting—the narrator sardonically comments: "It is not certain in what order he preferred them" (191). After making known the abysmal state of American "movies," the narrator awkwardly interrupts Guy Pollock's case against democratic mediocrity with similar opinions from an editor in Buenos Aires and a clerk in New York. Finally, part 3 ends in a burst of prophecy: "Then, for three years which passed like one curt paragraph, Carol ceased to find anything interesting save the Bjornstams and her baby" (224).

The narrator's decisive "ceased to find anything interesting" overstates the case but succeeds in setting the stage for some potent satire. Through Carol, Lewis assails the inanity, blatancy, sentimentality, and titillation of cinematic America. Vital to Main Street is the Rosebud Movie Palace, especially its showings of valiant Yankees in backward countries and of pie-throwing slapstick replete with showgirls. Lewis next makes merry with *The Girl from Kankakee* cast members, who act stagey, clown around at rehearsals, and deem Carol too "bossy" (218). While snickering at Gopher Prairie's tent-show tastes, Lewis also laughs at the banal optimism of community play-production manuals. On the eve of the sell-out performance, Lewis mocks the players who think of themselves as one with the footlight's long line of troupers. From the opening, Carol knows that the production is bad—just how bad Lewis's parody of the arty, slangy, chauvinistic, irrelevant, neighborly review in the *Dauntless* makes clear.

And the author continues to make his—and Carol's—attitudes patent by way of diverse cataloging. He inventories the salient features of Will's medical suite: shabby waiting room (which Carol makes habitable with rug, wicker chairs, and pictures) and cluttered all-purpose room. Lewis lovingly details Mrs. Bogart's antique-looking cottage, rebukingly neat and symmetrical, glutted with kitsch and religious photographs and odds and ends; besides pointing to her Sears, Roebuck catalog, he indexes her topics of tattle. A report on Nels Erdstrom's unsheltered but glossy white house constitutes evidence of the prospering farmer's social progress. Lewis juxtaposes Carol's memories of Mankato Christmases and the fine points of some of Will's hobbies. Though on their theater trip Carol judges the lading in the lobby of the grand Minneapolis hotel as "too florid" (206), she cannot help admiring its extravagance. Lewis catalogs the sight-seeing and the dining, the shopping and the window-shopping, typical of provincials in the metropolis. Finally, he records the nerve-racking doings at *Kankakee* rehearsals and the director's internal censures of the ongoing performance.

Carol's intellectual, emotional, and family pride enter cogently into the high-low, ideality-reality, climb-fall theme in this section. In their inaugural spat, Will asks Carol why she feels "so superior" (171). Taking the question literally, Carol defends her father's feeling of superiority to ordinary people. To her assumption of biological and environmental determinism, she reinforces place, the Mankato bluffs, where as a girl looking down on the tilted roofs she—like young Lewis—dreamed of writing poems. *There* the river valley collected her thoughts; *here* the open prairie scatters them.

Worth noting is Carol's recollection of the day that she and Will sat together on the sanctified heights of Fort Snelling: photographs of the Erdstrom farm and boy had lured her to Gopher Prairie. If there and then Carol tasted a liquor never brewed, the cocktail she drinks on her play-going trip to Minneapolis not only blunts her annoyance with the impertinent waiter but "elevate[s] her to a bridge among colored stars" (207). Perplexed by Dunsany's dramaturgy, Will later shatters her aesthetic transport as the stately Syrian queen on stage—for Mrs. Dr. Kennicott "fell with a jolt" (211).

Queen or no, Carol has determined early on never to have fat ankles and always to dress well. She observes that Mrs. Dillon's legs are as nice and slim as her own. Still, in preparing for bed, Carol (unlike Will) troubles to push aside the old plush chair and undress behind the closet door. This interjacence reappears in another form in the last section of *Main Street*. In Guy's office, Carol wonders if he fancies her new Oriental turban of rose and silver brocade, headgear expressive of her vague longings. At home, free association flourishes: a beaver coat to run her fingers over . . . fur as glossy as Guy's moustache. In moleskin cap, Carol, before calling on the censorious Widow Bogart, rubs off her lipstick. As she prepares for her theater trip, Carol discovers a hole in her one silk petticoat, beads missing from her chiffon-and-velvet frock, and a stain on her best crepe blouse—all of which permits her to rejoice in not having "a single solitary thing that's fit to be seen in." Down in Minneapolis, she invests in a rajah-silk frock, blouse, gloves, and a wool-flowered hat.

Granting her vanities about vesture, Carol's sympathies still run deep. She feels saddened by the sick and tired country people who must wait in Will's shabby office. She tries to raise a smile from the Erdstrom boy. She helps Will carry the sweating, stable-smelling Adolph Morgenrath to the kitchen operating table. In spite of her own and Will's "better" judgment, she aches for motherhood. In her quest for independence, she wishes not to hurt Will. In helping Will on his rounds, she finds great exhilaration. Awakening to the drama in her husband's driving by night to some distant farm, she asks herself: "What were her aspirations beside his capacity?" (175). But Lewis, here "doing up" Carol's latest coloring of reality as the doctor-hero's romanticizing wife, has not adequately foreshadowed the commonplaceness of a country doctor's middle-of-the-night calls.

At the Morgenrath farm, Carol's imagination is Bovaryesque: her heroically gruff husband is going to perform a miraculous surgical operation. "Oh, you *are* wonderful!" (188). Even a blizzard now—remembered as seen through a window with her father—is such stuff as dreams are made on. But unlike Mankato Christmases, Christmases in Gopher Prairie are not exciting. During this month of romance Carol is eager to understand Will's interests, but his random remarks and thinking aloud leave her unsatisfied, as does his view that romance is moonshine. To vary her days, Carol (no doubt in the manner of her father) dreams up little surprises, games, and gifts only to feel as betrayed by Will as she feels disillusioned by Guy, a "frame on which she had hung shining garments" (198). On the expanding evening of Jackson Elder's party, she falls into an "enchanted quietude." Carol has a premonition of "some great thing" coming to her (201). At the post-sledding party, she fancies herself foregoing domesticity by becoming riotously drunk; but so stirred is she by the game of charades that she cries out: "Let's form a dramatic club and give a play!" (203). On her moonlit way home, she imagines that she loves her friends, that she now is part of the community—the "great thing" has happened.

Carol daydreams later of sitting in a café in Brussels and going afterward to a little theater under a cathedral wall. Though Minneapolis is her Brussels and the Cosmos School of Music, Oratory, and Dramatic Art her gay little theater, the train trip nevertheless triggers Carol's vagary, and Lewis pulls out the stops. Carol is a young poet "attacking fame and Paris" (205). In the metropolis the young provincial wife feels free; Yeats and Dunsany transport her to other times, other places—until her husband's "Gosh all hemlock!" breaks the illusion (211). She is no longer queen . . . Will no longer striding youth. The jungle romance fades, but Lewis so fashions his effervescent Carol as to have her retain not only her easy dissatisfactions but also her fervor, her rush of feeling, her desire to create beauty by suggestion.

From Will, however, Carol wants something more explicit, more intellectually satisfying. Thanks to Pollock's disturbing allusion to the town's medical rivalry, Carol probes her husband until, his defenses down, he finally exposes Dr. Westlake as bogus, Dr. McGanum as bullheaded, and Dr. Gould as lazy. The new dentist, Dr. Dillon, is in league with Westlake and McGanum, whose wives are underhanded. Ironically, it is Will who charges Carol with an easy willingness to think the worst of Gopher Prairie: "Trouble with women like you is, you always want to *argue*" (166). Carol thinks, correctly, that the town expects her to accept its opinions without its accepting hers. She argues convincingly for a monthly allowance from her husband, but she does not follow through.

When she learns from Will that her questions, notions, and flightiness intimidate Sam, she defends her frankness and analyzes her superiority complex. In a disarming display of openness she then confesses her unfairness. Still, when Will points out that Jack Elder and Lyman Cass are "well-informed," Carol replies: "Gopher Prairie calls anybody 'well-informed' who's been through the State Capitol and heard about Gladstone" (171). In the boring vocabulary of land deals and motorcars she finds no soul-saving romance. But even when Lewis makes Carol sensible enough to say that Gopher Prairie is a market for farmers, not a stage for dramatists, he undercuts her complacency by having her overhear a disgruntled farmer complain: "Man, I'd like to burn this town down!" (223).

At times, the disillusioned Carol tries, without success, to free herself from all speculation. Her random thoughts and self-analyses resemble interior monologue. Guy is too old and reclusive for her to fall in love with. But she might if she were older. She questions her fidelity. Marriage has not changed her. She still yearns for the *idea* of Prince Charming. Will no longer stirs her. Still, if the *real* Prince Charming came, she would just look—and then run. She judges herself neither heroic nor fine, just a young vulgarian playing the misunderstood wife. She takes some satisfaction in not telling Guy about Will's faults, about his blindness to her remarkable soul. Because Carol comes to feel that Will's pulling one farmer through diphtheria is worth all her castle building, she informs Guy that he and she are "a pair of hypercritical loafers" (177).

Striking also is Carol's insight, after her visit to Auntie Bogart, into her own penchant for crusading: "But—isn't she just like me? She too wants to 'reform the town'! She too criticizes everybody! She too thinks the men are vulgar and limited! *Am I like her?* This is ghastly!" (183). And after watching Will operate, she tells herself: "And I thought that it was I who had the culture!" (188). Still, if Will were really her Prince Charming, would she not *demand* his child? Carol's thoughts as she lies in bed beside her sleeping husband remind one of Molly Bloom's ruminations in James Joyce's *Ulysses* (1922). As she inventories her daily life, she realizes that she no longer feels the thrill of being a doctor's wife. Carol's "I'm not trying to 'reform the town' now. . . I am trying to save my soul" seems a turning point (196). She now sees timid Guy Pollock as no messenger from the outside world but as belonging fully—his initials are suggestive—to Gopher Prairie.

Carol's original admiration for Guy flowed, of course, from his admiration for her—from his polite recognition, as Ambrose Bierce would cynically put it, of her resemblance to himself. If Carol is to Miles a sea gull, to Guy she is a hummingbird. To the Erdstrom boy she is an oddity; her fairy tale delights the boy far less than Will's bluff. Carol's own renewed delight in respect for Will quickly vanishes, however, after he mocks her discontent. "All of me left him when he laughed at me" (196). In Minneapolis Carol also becomes acutely aware of her diminishment when she self-consciously realizes that "no one was interested in her" (206). While one can smile at the schoolgirl for savoring the way a Blodgett professor once stared at her coiffure, one is less tolerant of the doctor's wife who buys an expensive silk dress and imagines a highly envious Juanita.

Equally disturbing are Carol's various shades of subterfuge. Only a "definite act of will" (160) enables her to tell her husband that since the Perrys were not in their apartment, she stopped in at Guy's office. Lewis enhances the romantic atmosphere of a chance encounter by the unlikelihood of Carol's not knowing that Guy and the Perrys share the same building. The remark that "doctors hate each other" Carol attributes not to Guy but simply to "some one" (165). Her theatrical work will partly and clandestinely "free" her (203), she hopes, from Will. Even away from Gopher Prairie Carol dissembles as she tries in Minneapolis to give the impression of a chilly elegance she does not feel. Back in Gopher Prairie, watching the performance of *The Girl from Kankakee* going down the drain, she understandably bolsters the players with "lying smiles" (221), a prefiguration of the *Dauntless* review, well-meaning but "so confoundedly untrue" (223).

To be sure, Carol is a smiler, but with no knife under her cloak. So confused is she by the urbanity of Minneapolis after her year and a half in Gopher Prairie that she actually seeks the serenity of the village. As earlier Guy had informed her, Gopher Prairie, after all, is friendly; unlike towns in Ohio, it will take in a stranger, if that stranger is politically and socially acceptable. Upon her return from Minneapolis, Carol learns that the second floor of the city hall (the old-time "op'ra house") is the town's only playhouse, excepting, of course, its photoplayhouse, the Rosebud Movie Palace. In the opera house or country theater of an earlier day, strolling players had performed such fare as *The Two Orphans, Nellie the Beautiful Cloak Model,* and *Othello.* But by Carol's time theater-in-a-can had already replaced the gypsy theater.

Lewis's display of local idiom in this section is particularly witty. In the nocturnal colloquy between Will Kennicott and a German-American farmer (and in the importuning letter the good doctor reads from another), Lewis makes plain that the immigrants have forgotten the language of the old country without learning the parlance of the new. As amusing as these exchanges (facsimiles of medical pidgin-German and agrarian fractured-English) is the author's pungent little red herring in-joke in the form of Mrs. Bogart's no-uncertain-terms reference to where the questionable waitress at Billy's Lunch should be sent: "to the school for the incorrigible girls down at Sauk Centre" (181). At Jackson Elder's lakeside shack, Lewis depicts the camaraderie of 20 Gopher Prairieites. Eating, drinking, and dancing, they say the same old things in the same old way, but Carol's suggestion that the group put on a play gives to the same old charades a new twist and thrust. At the first meeting of the 15-member Gopher Prairie Dramatic Association, seven show up. The rest send word that they will be at "all other meetings through eternity" (204).

The vows sound pious enough. But when Carol, upset by the tawdry rehearsals, appeals to the group's pride, satisfaction, "holiness," the ironic narrator points out: "In Gopher Prairie it is not good form to be holy except at church, between ten-thirty and twelve on Sunday" (219). What Carol herself feels on that moonlit winter night is, of course, consecration. Spiritually withdrawing from the babble, she enters into "a worship of incomprehensible gods" (201). She becomes one with night and the future, with mystery and the universe. Such mysticism contrasts sharply with her—and Guy Pollock's—attitude toward conventional Protestantism. Like Carol, Guy had also attended a denominational college. He affirms that God, after dictating the Word and hiring ministers, has been creeping around trying to catch disobeyers. In his life's final chapter, the lawyer foresees the preacher spinning lies over his lean dry body.

Again, the kitchen tête-à-tête between Carol and Guy about a more conscious life for more people has its less exalted counterpart in the living-room debate between Will and Vida about manual training for younger schoolchildren. Carol wants more than good taste and fastidious people. She thinks that women, workers, farmers, "Negroes," Asiatic colonies, and even some Republicans want a more conscious life. Identifying with them, Carol declares that they are tired of deferring hope to the next generation. "All we want is—everything for all of us!" (197). Unattainability naturally creates discontent. Hoping that Carol does not class herself with labor leaders who instigate strikes so that workers can buy junk, Guy believes that democracy in reality instead of in theory would reduce the world to moribund mediocrity. "You don't want to be mixed up in all this orgy of meaningless discontent," he warns (198). Disillusioned by Guy's political discretion, Carol sneers at her own ladylike taboos, her sense of social distinction that sees Miles and Bea as retainers and herself as Lady Bountiful.

Initially, of course, Carol looks on the highly cultured Guy as an attractive mystery. She delights in the literary incongruity of his office—amid his law books and newspapers the volumes of poetry, German novels, and even a Charles Lamb in crushed levant. Upon his arrival in Gopher Prairie, Guy had sworn to maintain his cultural interests, but too soon he senses the virulence of the village virus. For one Browning poem he reads four magazines of cheap fiction. When not giggling salaciously in Chicago over a copy of the *Parisienne,* he finds himself rereading in Gopher Prairie a Flandrau book he knows by heart. Serious reading in Gopher Prairie seems more duty than pleasure. Julius Flickerbaugh plows faithfully through *Literary Digest* and *Outlook.* Will plows faithfully through the *Journal of the American Medical Association.* He suspects that Dr. Westlake, who always has "an old Dago book" lying around, reads detective stories on the sly (161).

Though Will prefers to wait for a "regular" Broadway production, he consents to take Carol to her "darn foreign plays" (205) in

Minneapolis. On her way to the altar of Thespis, Carol, with only a sketchy knowledge of the turbulent Little Theater movement, buys books on the drama. The mummery in the unnamed Arthur Schnitzler play she perceives as stiff. In Bernard Shaw's trifling 1904 playlet, *How He Lied to Her Husband* (Will had hoped it would be racy), Carol appreciates the "conceit" of a husband who feels insulted that a young man claims *not* to have fallen in love with his beautiful wife. Though Carol's reading Yeats aloud had failed to make Will enjoy the poet—whom Lewis came to admire after hearing him lecture at Yale in 1903—she wants her husband to see *The Land of Heart's Desire* (1894). Carol, of course, is transported to the world of "thatched cottages," "green dimness," "linden branches," "twilight women," and "ancient gods" (210). Those familiar with the play will understand Carol's obvious identification with the young wife, Maire Bruin, who pleads:

> Come, faeries, take me out of this dull house!
> Let me have all the freedom I have lost;
> Work when I will and idle when I will!
> Faeries, come take me out of this dull world.[12]

After a shaky start, the unnamed Dunsany play transports Carol once more to another time and place. Sword-bitten doors of a crumbled palace . . . a caravan in the courtyard . . . elephants and camels from El Sharnak . . . orchid jungles beyond . . . a youth approaching the queen—until Will's disruptive commentary brings Carol back to Minnesota.

Lewis seems to have based this garbled one-act play on Dunsany's three-act *Laughter of the Gods* (1916), with its crumbled palace, caravan from Barbel-el-Sharnak, and orchid jungles. Of interest is a little scene in *Laughter of the Gods* between a pair of court ladies returning from a walk and another court lady named Carolyx. "O, We went down a little street," says one lady. "Yes, Yes," replies Carolyx. "The main street of the city," adds the other lady. "Yes, Yes, Yes," replies the eager Carolyx. "It ends in the jungle," concludes the first lady.[13]

Carol doubts that she will ever see the strange things of the world, yet she aspires to recreate them in plays. Vague, however, about precisely how to create beauty by suggestion, Carol decides on Shaw. Having already rejected Ella Stowbody's *Romeo and Juliet,* the five-member play-selection committee—Carol, Guy, Vida, Raymie, Juanita—act businesslike and artistic. Guy suggests the too commonplace *School for Scandal* and then the too difficult *Oedipus Tyrannus.* Vida recommends *McGinerty's Mother-in-Law,* a simple-minded high-school farce. When Carol makes her pitch for *Androcles and the Lion,* Guy supports her choice. Raymie, however, dispenses his usual Wutherspoonisms about the play's irreligion and lack of message and not leaving a nice taste in the mouth. When he advocates the instructive, inspirational, and syrupy *His Mother's Heart,* Juanita, in her best line in the novel, tells him to "Can the mother's influence!" (214). But since Carol's is the only nay vote to Juanita's proposal, *The Girl from Kankakee* carries the day.

Carol's dislike for the "classy" Broadway hit that she is to direct does not help matters. By reading and experimenting, she strains to be "furiously modern" (216), but she discovers, once more, that it is easier to imagine than to create sought-after effects. Some of the cast, kibitzing and skylarking, look upon their director (who in her infinite variety plays the maid) as tyrannical. After beholding an Ozark comedy, *Sunbonnet Nell,* in a "tent show" (219), Carol realizes that even *The Girl from Kankakee* will be too subtle for Gopher Prairie.

So galling to her is the looming performance that Carol feels like pitching it all. Her sensation here is in tune with her other escapist sentiments. Too often she protests that *if* Prince Charming came to Main Street she would flee from him. Cribbage with Will offers escape from the scandalizing Bogart, but when he ridicules his wife's "crank ideas" (196), Carol gives up her role as admiring hausfrau. *Main Street*'s shortest subsection—a 33-word still-life of one of Will's cigar-bands on top of Carol's dry violin (196)—is a striking objective correlative of the village virus. No longer able to find liberation through Guy (who refers to himself as a "living dead man" [155]), Carol finds only spotty release in the dramaturgy of Minneapolis and Gopher Prairie. During high-school commencement festivities, she feels old and detached and she broods on the possibility of never eluding the talk of tepid people. Though the reader is well aware of Carol's obsession with flight, Carol herself now is startled to discover that she is using the word "escape" (224).

Someday, thinks Guy Pollock, the kind of towns from which the Carol Kennicotts seek escape might be as obsolete as monasteries. A sort of secular monk himself, Guy envisions farmers and retailers speeding into charming cities by monorail (an idea first suggested by an English engineer back in 1826). Also surprising to young readers today is Guy's off-hand conviction in 1913 that if he doesn't stop smoking, cancer will get him at 50. Someday, Carol replies, the village virus might get her. Abruptly the utopian adds, "Someday I'm going—" (155). Meanwhile, she looks forward to her renewed career as a doctor's wife; Lewis has her no longer aspiring to build Aesthetica or even to play Rachmaninoff. But after Will's mockery, she speaks only of saving her own soul. Still, she thinks of children. And though Carol fears violence, she still wants adventure—along with nobility, the hearth, and someone to love as she goes on.

7

Mater Dolorosa

To some degree Carol finds some of the things she seeks in the three-chapter center section (19 through 21), part 4, which pivots on motherhood. Longing for people like herself, especially since Bea has left domestic service to marry Miles, Carol in chapter 19 serves on the library board, but she sees no vital change in her plodding life. At the summer cottage she indulges in escapist reveries about faraway places and imagines herself someday taking a train somewhere. As with the dramatic association and the library board, her turn to the Chatauqua brings further disillusionment. But in the light of the World War I and her "blessed event," life promises to become fervid.

In chapter 20, the precise center of *Main Street,* Carol becomes a mother. Lewis piles on precepts from Main Street, especially from Will's interfering Uncle Whittier and Aunt Bessie. Although devoted to her son, involved in child-welfare week, and seemingly settled down, Carol remains dubious and saddened by Gopher Prairie life.

Counterpart to her longing in chapter 19, the first picture in Lewis's triptych, is the third, chapter 21, a flashback revealing the secret longings of young Vida Sherwin; her early relationship with

Will; her true feelings about Carol; and, finally, at the suggestion of James Branch Cabell, her new relationship with Raymie.

Thus the novel's narrational omniscience comes into strong focus. The narrator opens chapter 19 with a one-sentence subsection about the next three years (1914–17) in Carol's public life and unchronicled longings. For two years she becomes part of the town, "one of Our Young Mothers" (236). At one point, the narrator overrides Carol's story to discuss the course of empire; Gopher Prairieites who leave town generally drift westward. During these three years Carol witnesses changes of face, not place. Lewis's narrator here sounds like some precursor to Thornton Wilder's nostalgic stage manager in that idealized microcosm, *Our Town* (1938). The narrator assures us that during these busy childrearing years, Carol devotes only a few minutes a day to her lonely desires. "It is probable that the agitated citizen has within his circle at least one inarticulate rebel with aspirations as wayward as Carol's" (242).

The most intrusive chapter in the novel, a bit of psychic slumming that cuts deepest into Carol's history, is, of course, chapter 21, Lewis's arresting portrait of Vida Sherwin's sexual fears, yearnings, and guilt. Much later, when Vida quizzes unheroic Raymie about his plans for a partnership in the Bon Ton, the ironic narrator reverts to giddy poesy: "He hymned the old unhappy wars in which he had been Achilles and the mellifluous Nestor, yet gone his righteous ways unheeded by the cruel kings" (251).

Raymie is unheeded by the Bon Ton kings, perhaps, but not by the enterprising 39-year-old schoolteacher in whose flattery the unheroic shoe salesman glows. The banality of their boardinghouse chit-chat is also fair game for Lewis's satire. But he derides even more the ambulant Chatauqua company that sells to intellectually proud Gopher Prairie a "solid week" of low-grade inspiration and entertainment (231). Lewis next blisters visiting in-laws, kith and kin who drop in uninvited and stay as long as they like. That the "Main Streetite" visits only places where he has relatives is a foregone conclusion. Thus the Smails hang on, first with Will's mother in Lac-qui-Meurt, and then with Will and Carol, until they decide to settle down in Gopher Prairie. Part and parcel of Lewis's satire of the pair are his accounts of their homespun incivilities toward Carol and her ideas. In contrast to these countrified uncouthnesses and the insipid Chatauqua program are the panoply of puerile topics that fall under the smug purview of Vida and Raymie.

At her first library meeting Carol discovers that the board is as egoistic about its little learning as she is about hers. She would even like to learn more of Will's land deal, but because he does not explain details, her interest is passive. She half expects, after her pregnancy, to sit and to talk unhappily ever after about babies, cooks, embroidery, and other mundanities. Meanwhile, she forebears public denunciations. Apparently unaware of their own mannerisms, Vida and Raymie take to task not only Carol's "flow of wild ideas" (249) but the "crazy way" she jumps from subject to subject (250).

Earlier at the summer cottage Carol escapes tedium through revery. Her mind battens on fiction read and pictures seen. She misses the trains chugging through Gopher Prairie, her assurance of a world beyond. Since the train itself is a form of village romance, and the conductors a special caste on a level with the Haydocks (but artist-adventurers apart), Carol melodramatizes the lonely night telegraph-operator, a Kafkaesque figure defying robbers and blizzards, heroically clicking messages out to and decoding messages in from the outside. She looks on brakemen and engineers as pilots of the "prairie sea" (230), an image made popular by James Fenimore Cooper. To the stillness of Carol's bed, Lewis brings the magical sound of the express, a sensation later made unforgettable by Thomas Wolfe. To take a train one day, Carol imagines, would be a "great taking" (231). Later the scent of Chatauqua dust, grass, and wood gives Carol the illusion, as at the Dunsany play, of Syrian caravans. Though Gopher Prairie satisfies Will, Carol finds pleasure in poring over maps and folders of Montana and Oregon.

Only to Vida, Raymie, and the Smails does Lewis grant the luxury of commenting on Carol's apparel—Vida and Raymie on Carol's new low shoes and proverbial turban and Uncle Whittier and Aunt Bessie on the "immodesty" of Carol's maternity gowns (236). Anatomical interest in part 4 centers on Carol shortly before and after Hugh's birth. Her predelivery and postpartum stands on motherhood surprise us; more surprising is Lewis's failure to represent a self-righteous Bogartian reaction to Carol's unholy complaints. Unexalted by the nuisance of the biological process, Carol of the doleful countenance cannot agree with the widow's exclamation that "being in a Family Way does make the girlie so lovely, just like a Madonna" (235).

Pregnant Carol feels unkempt, furious, sick, and bored. She notes her poor complexion, fallen hair, baggy shape, fallen arches, and uncommon fear that the baby *will* look like its parents. More shocking, she does not believe in maternal devotion. Though Will delivers babies routinely, Lewis is reticent about Hugh's birth, revealing only that Carol hates the baby for all the pain and fear he has caused. After the first day, however, she loves him with the devotion and instinct that proves the salaciously saccharine Bogart right, after all. Though alongside her baby Carol feels like a sandpaper-skinned old woman, she is nevertheless elated.

From Carol's heart also springs a high hope, symbolized by her son's patronymic. Without ado, the narrator informs us that the child "was named Hugh, for her father" (235). In 1917, Lewis named his first son Wells, in honor of the celebrated English writer H. G. Wells. Lewis once recorded his indebtedness to a kind graduate student, Hugh Rankin (who had counseled him at Yale), but in choosing a name for Carol's son (and by reverse extension Carol's father), the author of *Main Street* more likely had in mind another famous British writer whom he long admired, Hugh Walpole. Indirectly, Carol's sister also enters the centerpiece. Prying into a letter from her left on a table, Uncle Whittier insists ad nauseum that Carol should visit her more. In a novel replete with curious appellations, Lewis diminishes the import of Carol's vapid sibling and optician brother-in-law simply by leaving them nameless.

Playing Lady Bountiful, Carol manages to bring Will, Guy, and the Perrys to the wedding of Miles and Bea. As the narrator foretold in the first chapter of *Main Street,* Carol is not sullen to learn of the world's ability to be "casually cruel" (8), but she assuredly is dismayed. With white curtains, a canary, and a chintz chair, she helps Miles convert his shanty into a cottage. Only Carol's sickness and fear over her own pregnancy reduce her worry over the Bjornstams' struggles.

The weighty advice that Gopher Prairie dumps on young mothers is also a test of patience and sympathy. For not prizing the sum and substance of all that expostulation, Carol dislikes both herself and her benefactors. Though Carol, touched by the pitiful loneliness of the interfering Smails, resolves to be chilly to them, "she had no talent for conscious insolence" (239). Incredibly, Lewis would have the reader believe (by his mere mention) that Will's visiting mother—the reader never sees this phantom—stays two months with the Smails in Gopher Prairie, and that Carol likes her too much to insult her galling brother and sister-in-law. Overwhelmed by the baby's trust, Carol believes that she would sacrifice herself; still sympathetic to the plight of the world, however, she believes that she would not sacrifice other babies so that hers might have—the question goes begging—"too much" (235). During Will's charitable welfare week, she does double-duty. Besides loathing herself for not taking unasked-for advice, Carol feels the same emotion because of her class consciousness in taking Hugh to play with Olaf, especially when she sees how much Miles and Bea love both boys.

At Blodgett, one recalls, Carol did not yet know the ability of the world to be not only casually cruel but "proudly dull" (8). During her three years in Gopher Prairie, people come and go, but everything seems to Carol as unaltered as the surrounding fields. From the backbiting Bogart and the meddlesome Smails, Carol finds refuge with, of all company, the Jolly Seventeen. To the average denizen, the doctor's wife now seems no "traitor to the faith of Main Street" (242). After the new housekeeper's suspicion about her employer's frivolity wanes, the narrator informs us that the older woman adopts Carol as a daughter, but Oscarina's motherhood is small beer compared with the sisterhood Lewis created between Carol and Bea.

But an even greater contrast in the centerpiece is between true and false education. John Henry Newman makes the case in *The Idea of a University:* "Do not say, the people must be educated, when, after all, you only mean amused, refreshed, soothed, put into good spirits and good humour, or kept from vicious excesses."[14] After a week of Chatauqua, Gopher Prairie feels proud and educated. As Carol sees it, the facile instruction—stale entertainment and simplistic inspiration—seems to combine vaudeville, Y.M.C.A. lectures, and elocution exercises. When the final lecturer does, in fact, intelligently discourse on the town's "haphazard" architecture, the audience merely sheds his dark-sided "criticism" (233). But soon Carol broods less on her town's future than on her son's promise—at Harvard, Yale, or Oxford. One of the topics that Vida and Raymie chew on is Carol's "erroneous theory" that schools should not require "strict" discipline (249). Again, the question goes begging.

Besides regretting the Chatauqua superintendent's poetic infelicity, Carol listens to a shallow lecture opposed to profit-sharing. Her "new-fangled ideas"—many of which Lewis would have embraced—smell to the Smails like heresy (238). Formerly an independent tiller, Uncle Whittier rejects the notion of cooperation among farmers. That capitalistic distribution was unknown in the Garden of Eden the Smails look on as simply one of Carol's "funny ideas" (238). She, in turn, looks with delight on Miles playfully admonishing little Hugh to make his parents give him pants—"Join the union and strike" (240). Prompted by his own parenthood to set up child-welfare week, Will awards the best baby title to magnificent Olaf Bjornstam. Immediately and enviously the mothers speculate on the future of "that Swede brat," what with a hired girl for a mother and a cranky socialist for a father (241). If socialists tried to govern six months, speculate Vida and Raymie, the fallacy of their theories would be obvious.

Though Will earlier has briefed Carol on the town's readers, she is nevertheless surprised to discover at her first library-board meeting that Westlake quotes from *The Divine Comedy, Don Quixote, Wilhelm Meister,* and the Koran, and that Lyman Cass gleans the likes of Gibbon, Hume, Grote, and Prescott. Still, Carol sees that only she knows how to bring the library to the whole town. Unfortunately, the board is interested in what Carol regards as "old, stilted volumes" (226); unfortunately also, the patrons demand Henty books, Elsie books, and optimisms by moral women and virile clergymen. The rule of library silence Carol finds, perhaps too fatuously, antithetical to the principle of youthful volubility. The increased library-tax proposal goes down to defeat; and the board on the problem of the missing 17 cents resembles a knot of medieval metaphysicians on the capabilities of dancing angels. Budget problems compel Carol to withhold her recommendation for new purchases, 30 titles of which are recent European novels. After two frustrating years, Carol relinquishes her post to Vida.

Although holiness in Gopher Prairie is appropriate only in church on Sundays, the narrator speaks of the train in the West as a god, its tracks "eternal verities," its officials an "omnipresence," its romantic arrivals and departures the town's only mystery besides the Catholic mass (229). To dispel Biblical fuzziness, however, the droning Chatauqua superintendent inevitably lectures one morning on the Holy Land. Will hints about baptizing Hugh, but Carol refuses to ask the Baptist minister to sanction her child by way of "devil-chasing rites" (235). Out of Christian duty, the Smails, often inquiring into Carol's theology, admonish her to attend church every Sunday; after all, Aunt Bessie banally declares, God knows "a whole lot more" than the smartest folks know (238).

From the narrator's extended portrait of Vida Sherwin, we learn that her father had been a "prosy minister" and that she, like Guy and Carol, had attended a sanctimonious college (244). Reminding one of Sherwood Anderson's grotesquery in *Winesburg, Ohio* (1919), Lewis's going beyond his forte of exterior realism reveals young Vida dreaming of herself in a harem, praying passionately to the Son of God, and offering her own brand of Bovaryesque adoration. At age 34, the nun-like Vida, feeling sacrilegious for confusing her love for Jesus with her lust for the sporting bachelor Will, even buys a rosary but cannot bring her Protestant self to count beads.

Our insight into Vida's buried life and sexual sublimation allows us to understand why she is vexed by the unrepressed impatience of young Carol, whom she likes to think of as her and Will's child. Besides complimenting Raymie on his singing in the Episcopal choir and exchanging weather-talk with him at Methodist socials, Vida parleys with him at the boardinghouse on the value of eloquent sermons and the superiority of old solos like "Jerusalem the Golden." In keeping with his depiction of the couple's genteelism, the satirical narrator notes that the women at their Episcopal wedding wore "new kid slippers and long white kid gloves" (243).

The Kennicott lakeside cottage is not only a temporary escape from Gopher Prairie, but it is the setting for Carol's summer reveries, her "hundred escapes" (228). As Will had shattered her daydreams while watching plays in Minneapolis, so here he intrudes on her dreamy afternoons. One persistent imaginary scene, perhaps influenced by some bewitching impressionistic painting, is Mentone. "She stood on a terrace overlooking a boulevard by the warm sea" (228). In the ticking of a clock—fleeting time—she hears the sound of horse hoofs. The sound that Carol most misses at the lake, of course, is the train, both romantic symbol and real vehicle of escape. Like so many other escapees in the American novel—Dreiser's Carrie Meeber, Anderson's George Willard—Carol Kennicott dreams, as did the young Sinclair Lewis, of taking a train someday, somewhere.

As Carol earlier had turned to the dramatic association and then to the library board, so now she turns to the Chatauqua. And as she earlier had feared the trap of pregnancy, so now she realizes fully the trap of motherhood. For two years Carol broods on her child, manages to be part of the town, and "had no apparent desire for escape" (236). The operative word here is *apparent.* In imagining Hugh someday leaving Gopher Prairie, Carol finds vicarious escape, but in time the old yearnings return and Carol again feels "trapped" (240), kidnapped by the town, finding respite in Juanita's gay gossip, in the Jolly Seventeen's united laughter at the Widow Bogart. Eventually Carol feels so trapped, however, that she gladly would move—simply for change, simply for the look and promise of adventure—to another Main Street.

At the first meeting of the library board, Carol harbors plans to "revolutionize the whole system" (226). But she changes nothing; and at the lake she believes that nothing will ever change. The truly great thing someday would be for her to take a train. But in the peril of great change—the coming of war and her baby—life at last, she believes, will prove interesting. Her reason now for living is Hugh and his promise. As Carol looks to the future, she foresees that he shall have everything, but he will not always be here in Gopher Prairie. Only a few minutes each day now do her own frustrated aspirations rise from below the surface of village life.

8

Village Intellectual

As Carol grows closer to herself and to her son, she feels in the next six chapters, part 5 (chapters 22 through 27), her growing estrangement from her husband and from Gopher Prairie. Using Carol as his mouthpiece on the village in American literature, on the Americanization of immigrants, on aggressive mediocrity, and on universal standardization, Lewis resorts in chapter 22 to a contrivance that too easily eliminates that art which conceals art. While their husbands attend a lodge inauguration in Wakamin, Vida stays overnight with Carol, who unloads her critical freight train.

Carol's spiritual dying at home in chapter 23 parallels the bloody sacrifice overseas. As fearful of revolution as is Cy Bogart of the draft, Carol at long last meets Gopher Prairie's darling son, millionaire Percy Bresnahan, president of the Velvet Motor Company. Though she dislikes his presumptions and his opinions, he makes her feel desirable. Increasingly irritated by Will, Carol in chapter 24 arranges a room of her own and even confides in pussyfooted Mrs. Westlake. Carol is vexed further by Oscarina's leaving, by Will's plans for a new house, and by her short trip with him to Joralemon.

Chapter 25 treats the onset of Will's affair with voluptuously sallow Maud Dyer, while Carol, all innocence, proclaims his fidelity. While Will obtains solace in calls on neurotic Maud, Carol and Hugh in chapter 26 feel jubilation by visiting the Bjornstams—until Bea and little Olaf die of typhoid. In the heavy-handed irony of chapter 27, effete Raymie Wutherspoon, victorious in war, becomes a captain of infantry, while tough-minded Miles Bjornstam, defeated by Gopher Prairie, moves to Canada. In another highly ironic episode, Carol is shocked when eccentric Mrs. Julius Flickerbaugh confides that she has hated Gopher Prairie for 32 years. Thus the author keeps Carol and the reader waiting . . . for something.

Carol's series of verbal essayettes in chapter 22 subserve Lewis's pamphleteering here, more sociological than artistic. The narrator indicates that the feelings are Carol's, but the sheer fluidity and expressive power are his own. Though Carol realizes that she is better off than many other women, the narrator points out: "It has not been recorded that any human being has gained a very large or permanent contentment from meditation upon the fact that he is better off than others" (255). Thus in his analyses of the literary village, Americanization, mediocrity, and standardization, Lewis's omniscient narrator simply holds forth, interspersing phrases like "asserted Carol," "said Carol," and "Carol insisted," but soon, losing even this scant distance, he writes: "Carol's small town," "She had remembered," and "behind her comments." The narrator winds up with, " 'There we are then,' said Carol," and drops her back into dialogue with Vida (255–61). As for Carol and Hugh's adventures at the Bjornstams', the omniscient narrator explains: "She did not quite understand it herself; did not know that in the Bjornstams she found her friends, her club, her sympathy, and her ration of blessed cynicism" (305).

Prominent cataloging in part 5 of *Main Street* treats Carol's lonely daily routine, the things Gopher Prairie thinks about, the ugly features of American small towns, and graphic details of the ugly Kennicott kitchen. After all of this, Lewis compiles an effective list of disclosures that Carol makes to the receptive Mrs. Westlake. He then inventories the silly attractions at the Beavers Fair in Joralemon.

The idealism/height motif emerges when Carol, in analyzing Gopher Prairie's militant mediocrity, explains to Vida that the community ideal is cheap kitchen labor and increasing land values, "not the grand manner, the noble aspiration, the fine aristocratic pride" (260). Only in the lowly cottage of the three Bjornstams do Carol and Hugh find "high adventure" (305).

Though 30-year-old Carol gladly feels old next to her son, she resents feeling old next to a "visibly" younger Vida. In the bathroom mirror, Carol scrutinizes her "pallid" face, "sharper" nose, and "granulated" neck (265). Still, Bresnahan makes her feel "young and soft" as he eyes her lips and shoulders (277). Apropos of Uncle Whittier's judgment earlier on Carol's maternity gowns is his "Hee, hee, hee" (as lascivious as any emanation from Cy Bogart) that her dress looks "kind of low in the neck" (279). But more revealing than décolletage to weary Carol is the realization that no longer is she the girl in breeches and flannel shirt who five years earlier had cooked over a Rocky Mountain campfire.

Only her youthful imagination seems unchanged. The fantastic, the nebulous, and the distant are to her as a child's airborne playmates. But beyond recall now is Carol's own early bridal pride. Thus she wonders how the hearth can fulfill Vida. Loathing unimaginative standardization, she identifies with Scandinavian "foreignness" and laments the ironing out of colorful immigrant food, dress, and song (258). When Vida calls her an "impossibilist" (263), Carol temporarily forsakes her phantom Frenchman, Strindberg, and classical dance in some phantom Gopher Prairie. While passengers behold outside their train windows a decorous small-town woman planting bulbs around the station, the woman, Carol Kennicott, imagines herself running garlanded through Babylon. Gopher Prairie offers her nothing strange and beautiful.

From the manly Bresnahan, however, she learns that she is a not uncommon type of rebel, and her reluctant admiration for the magnate compels her to study her husband, "to perceive the strangeness of the most familiar" (277). Summoning up the sacrality of her courtship, she doubts that Will's poker chums could ever comprehend her fragile world, which makes her suspect both herself and her world. Yearning for a trip east after Bresnahan's "disturbing flavor of travel and gaiety" (291), Carol imagines herself visiting Emerson's manse, bathing in a jade and ivory surf, meeting an aristocratic stranger. One thinks of Lewis's excited first visit to Concord in 1904, of how closely Carol's surf resembles a Japanese print, of the resemblance between her romantic whim and Emma Bovary's romantic obsession.

On the freight caboose to Joralemon, Carol pretends that she and Will are traveling again to the Rockies. Radiant with holiday illusions, she stares at the houses in Joralemon, only to discover that they are like the houses in Gopher Prairie. But just how blind Carol can be to her husband's "transparent" mind Lewis makes plain when Aunt Bessie and Auntie Bogart come gossiping about local sexual improprieties. In making up stories for Hugh, Carol also seems under the illusion that she is discovering the soul of things. When not playing disreputable minstrels with Hugh by secretly visiting the Bjornstams, Lewis's Carrie often muses alone, like Dreiser's Carrie, in a rocking chair.

The intellectual upshot of all her brooding is her one-woman judicial inquiry. The judge's daughter indicts Gopher Prairie as the type of the deadening American small town. Her thoughts, Carol passionately tells Vida, are the thoughts of women in 10,000 Gopher Prairies. All western villages exhibit standard frontier-camp flimsiness: streets too wide and too straight, structures rectangular, colors sober, hills without homes, views blocked by the railroad, creeks dumped into. "Diversity" is but another name for "conformity." For all his casual heroism, even Will is as standardized a doctor as Gopher Prairie is a standardized town, which exists (Carol indeed has read her Veblen) to make money from the farmers. The beginning of the remedy, if any, might be criticism; if nothing can help much, sympathetic attacks might help a little.

Carol's assault, while thoughtful, is seldom profound. The production of cheap utility, for example, is an American miracle, but she does not see this. For Carol, the world's chief end is not savorless people, mechanical talk, tasteless food, inane decorations, and mechanical music. In the uniform grayness of "Americanization," in the exchange of ancient fjord songs for "She's My Jazzland Cutie," Carol rightly sees loss, not increment. To be "intellectual" or "artistic" in such a world is to be regarded by those who see themselves as the greatest race on earth as priggish and of dubious virtue (258).

Lewis's attitude toward the "intellectual" and the "artistic" was as ambivalent as his attitude toward Carol and, if he detected any signs of affectation, altogether caustic. Particularly abhorrent to Carol is Main Street's serene pride of ignorance. And altogether false to her are the two traditions of the small town in the popular literary imagination: Friendship Village and Local Color. Unforgettable is this bit of blistering Lewisiana out of Carol's mouth: "It is an unimaginatively standardized background, a sluggishness of speech and manners, a rigid ruling of the spirit by the desire to appear respectable. It is contentment . . . the contentment of the quiet dead, who are scornful of the living for their restless walking. It is negation canonized as the one positive virtue. It is the prohibition of happiness. It is slavery self-sought and self-defended. It is dullness made God" (257).

As Carol believes that small towns are universally dull, mean, bitter, nosy, and timid, so she believes that the American village is taking pains to become as standardized and pure, as mediocre and bully-minded, as Victorian England. Unable to swallow Carol's ideas, Vida conveys her own stalwart efforts to build the town, and Carol admits to being no Spartan wife. As she later tells Bresnahan, Main Streetites endure because they don't know what they are missing; were she living in a city, she at least would have other Carols to play with.

Vigorous play, indoors or out, is still important to Carol. The picnic at Red Squaw Lake, however, is less backdrop for her outdoorsmanship than for Bresnahan's confident oratory. When later this Dreiserian Strong Man pats her hand on their drive up to Lake Minniemashie, she responds neither to him nor to the countryside. In the quaint caboose to Joralemon with Will, however, she revels in the freight's slowness through lakes and fields. Exhilarated, she shouts to Will and the Calibrees in Joralemon: "Let's be wild! Let's ride on the merry-go-round and grab a gold ring!" (295). But she returns to Gopher Prairie depressed, without the ride and grab. Carol's ambition to be in bed by nine stems in part from the aches of her housework.

Still, when free of pain, she likes the reality, the lively hours, of physical exertion.

Her pain, however, makes her not only cynical about the simple life of labor but even more sympathetic to the world's toilers. And though unhappy herself, Carol is sympathetic to Vida Wutherspoon's happiness. Vida, in turn, wonders how anyone like Carol, with no sympathy for Gopher Prairie, can hope to do anything for it. Carol counters that her fuming is a sign of affection, and to show her good will she gathers in not only the Campfire Girls but funds for a village nurse for the poor. Carol's botanizing with Hugh reaffirms her love for life's plenitude. She is touched by Raymie's itch for heroism, but Vida's rejoinder makes her feel impertinent. Unlike other Red Cross volunteers, Carol cannot roll hate for the enemy into the bandage she makes. While her marriage deteriorates, she yet feels for Will "an admiring affection" (266). Thus she is as shocked to realize that she no longer "definitely" looks at Will (280) as she is to realize that she never really looks at the "sty" of the maid's room in the old Kennicott place (287). Strengthened by her great love for Bea and Olaf, fragile Carol is able to nurse them from morning until midnight for a week.

But before this great trial, Carol sees herself as enfeebled by guilt, loneliness, and rebellion. She blames herself for not rejoicing, like homemaking-hungry Vida, in domestic chores. Feeling that her "superior" loneliness is, after all, a misfortune, she senses that the Main Street mediocrity that levels the immigrants is also flattening her. Probably Bresnahan *could* seduce her, she thinks, though she could not long abide his buoyancy, hypocrisy, and bullying. She discerns that her rudeness to him and to others is only self-defense. Fuming after an argument with Will, she rashly divides the world into two races: his calls hers "neurotic" and hers calls his "stupid" (284). Again, like a forerunner of Molly Bloom, Carol introspectively reviews her relationship with her husband: "We'll never understand each other, never; and it's madness for us to debate—to lie together in a hot bed in a creepy room—enemies yoked" (284).

To be sure, Carol finds that living a lie, that outwardly conforming to Main Street's good examples and standards of duty, is painful—especially since she believes that those who want her to believe that

Gopher Prairie is sufficiently beautiful and strange are themselves lying. Also painful to Will is his living a lie, his clandestine affair with Maud Dyer—especially since he earlier rejected roué Nat Hicks's conviction that "What they don't know won't hurt 'em none" (302).

Ever susceptible to the attitudes and feelings of others, Carol still seeks admiration. She even fears, in the event of a proletarian takeover, that the "common people" she happens to love would no longer regard her as Lady Bountiful (267). Despite her better knowledge, she is puffed up by Main Street's envy of how much the Kennicotts sport with the great Bresnahan. Besides arguing effectively, he is so successful that Carol, though his ideological adversary, does not want him to despise her—as Bresnahan, for example, despises Miles, whose gratuitous impudence he stingingly rebuffs. For confiding in suave Mrs. Westlake Carol finds no admiration from Will, but she does win his shy praise when, maidless, she proves deft at housework.

Carol's critical tour de force on the American village, however, receives no plaudits from Vida. In Carol's view Gopher Prairie no longer thinks in the quaint terms of local-color hoss-swapping (the stage Yankee comes to mind) but in the standardized language of gadget-buying modernity. America's leaders are jumbo versions of its small-town businessmen, bankers, and lawyers. In carbon-copy towns (lacking the international mind and the scientific spirit), Carol sees "dull safety" (260). Her—Lewis's—generalities come sweeping and glittering. Unlike stately capital cities, says Carol, towns offer nothing in return for their parasitism. Her later discovery that Joralemon indeed is a replica of Gopher Prairie substantiates her analysis. So vivid is Lewis's initial picture of downtown that by merely alluding in part 5 to its ugly low shops creeping down Main Street and to Carol walking her unvarying route he evokes the tedium of the quotidian.

When doing her own daily housework Carol especially broods on the inhabitability of the old Kennicott haunt, its nicked and spotted china, damp kitchen, battered utensils. The roost above the kitchen, Will points out, is better than anything hired girls have back on the farm. Planning someday to build a "real" house (288) around a "crackajack" furnace (289), Will looks upon Carol's architectural beau ideal as "overdone" (288). Carol, in turn, views his as monotonous as Sam Clark's square yellow clapboard. To assert his individuality—or conformity in diversity—Will declares for no "fool tower" and "flashy yellow"—a "nice cream" perhaps or maybe even shingles in a "nice brown stain" (288). After the Smails add their mite, Will sketches his quite standardized habitat, with particular attention to the garage. When Carol suddenly discerns picturesqueness in the old Kennicott "rookery," Will simply sets his plans aside (290).

For most Gopher Prairieites, however, the chief reason for setting aside plans is the war. Here Lewis pricks a few myths about loyalty and sacrifice. Some Main Streeters suspect German-Americans of disloyalty and draft dodging. To be sure, some of the town's leading citizens are at the front, but most Gopher Prairie soldiers are sons of German and Swedish farmers. The town's only officers are Dr. Gould, Dr. McGanum, and Raymie Wutherspoon. Since Will is the only "youngish" physician left in the area, the council of doctors, elevating ritual patriotism above rivalry, requests that Will not enlist unless needed (266). In what the narrator terms "tragicomedy," a succession of wartime hired girls passes through the Kennicott house (286). Unlike Bea who married and Oscarina who returned to help out at the farm, most farmers' daughters now flee to the city. There they find better jobs and personal freedom.

Carol meanwhile is as oppressed as ever by not only village dullness but by Vida's relentless educationalism. She charges, rightly, Carol with doing less for the town than the people she laughs at. Sam Clark, for example, works for better school ventilation. And for years Vida and Superintendent Mott have been "dinging away at the moneyed men" until they promise to vote the bonds for a big modern school. "We didn't call on you because you would never stand the pound-pound-pounding year after year without one bit of encouragement" (263). Ashamed, Carol yet feels compelled to ask if teachers in the new building will instruct in the same old uninspired way. And though she complies with Vida's invitation to direct the Campfire Girls, Carol is concerned less with coaching them to become good wives than in bringing into their dingy world the "subversive color" of Sioux dances (264).

At one point during Carol's own incendiary dance of intellect, Lewis's piety bashing again becomes apparent. Upon hearing her allude to the rector, Vida interrupts Carol's disquisition with the comic-relief notification that Ray—not *Raymie*—would have made a "wonderful rector." He has, to wit, a religious soul and reads the service beautifully. "As I tell him," Vida adds anticlimactically, "he can also serve the world by selling shoes and—I wonder if we oughtn't to have family-prayers?" (259). Though Vida faults Carol for sneering at religion, it is Carol who is shocked when Red Cross workers speak not of God and men's souls but of trivia and atrocity. While Carol would like the Scandinavians to preserve their customs, Bresnahan hands out checks to churches that promote Americanization. Miles informs Carol that he once heard a sermon of misinformation on evolution at the Methodist Church. Small wonder, since as late as 1927 a bill prohibiting discussion of evolutionism in Minnesota public schools was not defeated, simply indefinitely postponed. Miles also confesses that his agnostic jokes offend Bea's Lutheran friends.

Like cranky Miles, Carol is not only an agnostic who steps on "pet religious corns" (307), but she also dips, as noted, into Thorstein Veblen. While newspaper headlines now satisfy Vida, Carol still reads books, borrowed and bought. Besides Veblen, she consults other "subversive" writers (256) whom Lewis dearly catalogs: Anatole France, Romain Rolland, Martin Andersen Nexö, H. G. Wells, G. B. Shaw, Ellen Key, Edgar Lee Masters, Theodore Dreiser, Sherwood Anderson, and H. L. Mencken. The student of this period might well imagine the pull on Carol of, say, France's *Life of Joan of Arc* (1908) and *The Revolt of the Angels* (1914), Rolland's *Jean-Christophe* (1904–12), Nexö's *Ditte* (1917), Wells's *Tono-Bungay* (1908) and *The History of Mr. Polly* (1910), Shaw's *Major Barbara* (1905), Key's *Love and Marriage* (1911) and *The Woman Movement* (1912), Masters's *Spoon River Anthology* (1915), Dreiser's *Sister Carrie* (1900) and *Jennie Gerhardt* (1911), and Mencken's *A Book of Prefaces* (1917), this last containing a long essay—"Puritanism as a Literary Force"—that influenced Lewis mightily. One would prefer to see Carol reading Anderson's *Winesburg, Ohio,* but since this celebrated work was not published until 1919, one might imagine her reading *Windy McPherson's Son* (1916).

Such reading prompts Carol to study Main Street. Though, again, she finds only two literary traditions of the American small town—Friendship Village and Local Color—actually there is another. One is puzzled that a reading librarian like Carol has not yet found the antivillage tradition, which begins with Edward Eggleston's *The Hoosier Schoolmaster* (1871), gathers strength with E. W. Howe's *The Story of a Country Town* (1883) and Joseph Kirkland's *Zury: The Meanest Man in Spring County* (1887), and attracts much attention with Hamlin Garland's *Main-Travelled Roads* (1891) and Harold Frederic's *The Damnation of Theron Ware* (1897). The twentieth century formulates the "revolt from the village" tradition beginning with *Spoon River Anthology,* which Carol evidently *has* discovered. Several fine novels in the antivillage tradition—Anderson's *Poor White* and, as earlier noted, Floyd Dell's *Moon-Calf* and Zona Gale's *Miss Lulu Bett*—were published in the great literary year of 1920—the year Carol's story ends and Lewis's masterwork appeared.

Despite her fling in the little theater, Carol still bemoans the absence in Gopher Prairie of Strindberg plays, classic dance, and—silliest of all—a cynical, black-bearded, hand-kissing, Rabelaisian Frenchman. Although Carol would prefer Strindberg, she patiently listens to Ethel Clark divulge the plot of a magazine serial about a Turkish dancer. Though in the beginning Will had read certain books to impress Carol, he doesn't want to talk incessantly about Longfellow. "You've fussed so much with these fool novels and books and all this highbrow junk—you like to argue!" (284). Lewis makes altogether plain the country doctor's insensibility to the injunctions of art when he has an exasperated Will declare that Carol "ought to of been an artist or a writer or one of those things" (297).

Besides reading Eugene Field to Hugh, fashion-conscious Carol reads *Vogue,* the magazine for which Grace Hegger worked when Lewis first met her. The women's magazines ("with high-colored pictures and optimistic fiction") that Vida, Maud, and Mrs. Zitterel take to the dying Bea point up the pathos of her situation and the vanity of their gifts (310). After Bea and Olaf die, Guy Pollock becomes for

Carol merely a pleasant voice saying things about "Charles Lamb and sunsets" (312). Finally, it is the eccentric Mrs. Flickerbaugh who asks Carol if she can be satisfied only with reading.

If in the world of most readers "well satisfied is well paid," the same cannot be said about the world of most workers. Only the farmers, as Carol sees it, are politically adventurous. The parasitic townspeople mock as "cranks" and "half-baked parlor socialists" those who support cooperative experiments (259). Farmers someday might own their own market towns, Carol speculates, but she herself has no reform program, for she now sees the economic problem as basically spiritual, unsolved by leagues or political parties. She is made uncomfortable by the unpatriotic Miles, who sees the Great War as boss-directed fighting among workers. The thought of millions of Miles Bjornstams taking over the country frightens her. But by having conservative Percy Bresnahan, with his "inside of the inside" information (272), trumpet that Reds in power would be worse than a German king and that the exiled Russian czar will be back in power before year's end, Lewis effectively damages the local wizard's credibility. Bresnahan's words on outside agitators at his plant echo Jackson Elder's at his mill. The big man's rugged name-calling and nimble counterattacks on experiments in state socialism and "long-haired adenoidal nuts" confuse Carol, who believes that government control and labor organization would make not for inept experimentation but for scientific correction.

That Carol does not have a sense of the complex interrelationship of things, especially of custom, is clear. To little Hugh Kennicott, the Red Swede who runs up a ladder, waves his hammer, and sings "To arms, my citizens" is a world hero (306). If workers had a cooperative bank, Miles tells Carol, they would not need Stowbody. Again, needing Oscar Eklund's water but not his insults ("Sure, you socialists are great on divvying up other folks' money—and water!" [309]), Miles, proud but as yet well-less (and seemingly more anarchist than socialist), turns imprudently to the contaminated hollow water.

These waters, of course, give to mother and son not life but, at Cabell's suggestion, death, their doom coming in the context of lethargy at home and carnage abroad. Carol's street is "meshed in silence . . . conversation starting and dying . . . a street beyond the end of the world . . . beyond the boundaries of hope . . . tediousness made tangible . . . a street builded of lassitude and futility" (314). Lewis's early description of Poplar Street on a hot summer night makes Guy Pollock's village virus palpable. The description seems even to carry overtones of the famous "etherized" evening in "The Love Song of J. Alfred Prufrock" (1915); besides unmistakable resemblances between Sinclair Lewis's Pollock and T. S. Eliot's Prufrock, Carol Kennicott feels that for the past five years she has been "under ether." Waking in the middle of the night to "hovering death," she examines her pallid face in the mirror, as noted earlier, and thinks that as she grows older, Vida (Spanish for *life*) grows younger. Carol wonders if time simply will "slink past" until she dies. She assumes a quasi-solipsistic posture: "When I die the world will be annihilated, as far as I'm concerned" (265). Before her demise, she wants (tiresomely, one must add) the sea and ivory towers.

Now that men and women are dying, Vida wants Carol to be less critical, more patriotic. Both Miles and Carol want the Prussian autocracy defeated, but the village radical discomforts her when he speaks of America exporting democracy—the democracy of death. As the shifts of war oblige Carol to do more of her own housework, she imagines the "death-rimmed years" of millions of women (287); and she fears moving into a new house in Gopher Prairie, for "there she would die" (290). In his treatment of typhoid, Lewis's details on the degeneration and death of Olaf and Bea are striking; the episode, however, is marred by Dickensian sentimentality, even bathos, as when delirious Bea "did not know that Olaf would no longer swing his lathe sword on the door-step, no longer rule his subjects of the castle-yard! That Miles's son would not go East to college" (310–11). And though Carol helps the father wash the bodies of his wife and child, she is too prostrated to attend the pathetic but improbable funeral at which Miles Bjornstam is the sole mourner. Like some latter-day Leatherstocking, he strikes out for some less populated place in Canada, another illustration of escape from Main Street.

Hundreds of thousands share Miles's discontent with small-town life, but flee to the city instead. According to Carol's research, they seldom return. From the terrifying gales and the grim rectangularity of Gopher Prairie, however, Carol herself sees "no escape" (260). When Bresnahan places his arm around her waist, she retreats to Hugh's room, ahead of him and Will. And when the automobile pasha later proclaims her good fortune in living in his hometown, she replies: "You don't have to stay. I do" (275). The better to stay, Carol fashions out of the spare chamber a room of her own. To this bookish sanctuary she repairs when upset by Will or the Smails. Although she tells Mrs. Westlake about the need to separate from men, "to get off and laugh at them" (286), she finds vicious her own doubts about the sanctity of family life. Still, in the new standardized house that Will plans to build, Carol sees the "swing doors of a prison" (290). Sad to say, she flies from Will's intimacies until he himself feels like an outsider in his own home.

In him Carol does not see the glamour of her son's unknown future, the future on which the mother spins dreams—until fearful images of routine and loneliness intrude. Every year since her marriage Carol had longed for a trip east, but every year Will had good reason not to go. With each passing year her desire to go increased. At one point, Carol suggestively jokes: "I think baby and I might up and leave you, and run off to Cape Cod by ourselves!" (291).

9

American Bovary

Before mother and child "up and leave" Gopher Prairie, Lewis in part 6 (chapters 28 through 33) treats Carol Kennicott's uneasy romance with handsome Erik Valborg, the new tailor in town. Seeing Erik as highly attractive, she resents the town's jokes about the "needle-pusher" (315). Meanwhile, she finds a new friend in the frivolous young schoolteacher, Fern Mullins. After talking to the tailor, she decides to make him—Keats in Gopher Prairie!—her new cause, to defend him against village mistreatment. To tangle matters, Lewis has Carol see in the admiring youth her dear father's image. After observing the disreputable Mrs. Swiftwaite, a milliner, Carol suspects her own motives regarding Erik. Still, on a picnic she withdraws with him from the high jinks of Cyrus, Fern, and the Dyers.

Full of self-pity, Carol hates both herself and the watching town. When Erik confesses his love, Carol balks; and when he kisses her in her husband's absence, she—unlike the Continental Madame Bovary—dismisses him. She imagines catastrophic happenings to Will and senses Main Street leering at her. When Mrs. Bogart accuses Fern of corrupting Cy, Carol looks upon the young schoolteacher as a surrogate victim and tries to protect her reputation after the girl reveals

Cyrus's drunken and lewd behavior; the school board, however, invites Fern to resign. After Will, interrupting Carol and Erik on a country walk, chastises his wife at home, Erik flees to Minneapolis. To cap the end of the romance (and to parallel Mrs. Bogart's assault on Fern Mullins), Erik's father accuses Carol of corrupting his son. She and Will close ranks by preparing for a trip to California. As the train leaves Minneapolis, Carol imagines her nearness to Erik for an hour.

Though the intrusive and abusive narrator militates against the novel's "realism," Lewis holds fast to this interpretative device. When Fern invites the Kennicotts to chaperon the little preschool picnic spree for herself and Cyrus ("he's a brat but he's lively"), Carol accepts, declining for Will and suggesting the Dyers as fellow chaperons (342). When Fern, in turn, suggests that Erik be invited, the narrator affirms: "So the picnic of Carol, Fern, Erik, Cy Bogart, and the Dyers was not only moral but inevitable" (343). At the Haydocks' lawn party, Carol, jealous of Erik and Myrtle Cass's gaiety, not only "nodded cooly" but, adds the narrator parenthetically, "she was proud of her coolness" (351). When, to keep watchful eyes later from seeing her and Erik on the porch, Carol invites him inside, the narrator remarks that "it is women who are the calm realists once they discard the fetishes of the premarital hunt" (354). When Vida accuses Carol of always playing, of not knowing true suffering, the narrator cites as two unendurable insults (1) that a person has no sense of humor and (2) that a person has never seen trouble. Not permitting the reader to miss the evil in bogywoman Bogart's "obscene wallowing" and assault on Fern Mullins, the narrator declares: "The gutter comedy turned into high tragedy, with Nemesis in black kid gloves. The actual story was simple, depressing, and unimportant. As to details Mrs. Bogart was indefinite, and angry that she should be questioned" (364).

Besides satirizing the town's techy snooper, Lewis has Carol see the woman's Christianity as a "sanguinary and alien theology," the Baptist Church itself "half barn and half Gopher Prairie parlor" (317), wherein the congregation sings inane hymns and heeds the incoherent sermons of the lilac-tied Reverend Zitterel, an "intense young man with a bang" (318). In his depiction of the impromptu lakeside picnic,

Lewis ridicules Dave's clowning, Maud's mawkishness, and Cy's tricks, those of "a gangling twenty-year-old satyr" (344). At the church-basement supper the Baptists, Lewis notes, "had doffed their piety" (348). Here Erik, begging to be liked, too expressively tries to charm all the girls, and Carol is sad for him. The satire in this section concludes with Lewis's demolition of Jolly Seventeeners on the finer points of hotel stays.

His cataloging in this section exposes Gopher Prairie's less visible open secrets. Lewis characterizes the sartorial-pornographic hash in Nat Hicks's rolltop desk. From the rear window of Nat's shop, Carol surveys Main Street's dirty and dismal backside of rot, pulp, grease, flies, and manure. Erik, noticing this vista as little as possible, informs his disgusted visitor that he is "learning to look inside" (339). As Carol's infatuation for the young tailor grows, Lewis itemizes facets of the world under lamplight and in sunshine that give Carol pleasure, felicity dispelled when the author records Carol's fears of what particular townspeople (as well as the barbershop and pool-parlor crowd) are thinking about her and Erik. When Carol hastens to the Minniemashie House to comfort Fern, Lewis graphically delineates the stale smells, sickly walls, and grim furnishings of Gopher Prairie's "sanctuary of hospitality" (368).

While revealing the Lady Bountiful in his central character as bowing to Bea, Miles, and Fern, Lewis maintains tenacious Carol's sense of herself as high-bred. The judge's daughter/doctor's wife tells herself that she would not care to socialize with a "capering tailor" (324). But when Erik Valborg suggests staging Susan Glaspell's psychoanalytical satire, *Suppressed Desires* (1914), a disarmed Carol decides to stop patronizing him. Yet old habits die hard, and she later advises him "loftily, rather discursively" (329), about his intellectual and emotional shortcomings; the young man's humility so humbles her, however, that she wonders if *she* is not the naif. Still, Lewis has her show up at Erik's tennis to-do "as embarrassed and agreeable as the bishop's lady at a Baptist bazaar" (334). Later she idealizes her destination as joyous universal youth—which Erik represents and to whom she wishes to impart "high, improving things" (348). To her husband she proclaims that some day Erik will be great. Further, she charges her husband with encouraging the people of Main Street "to drag me down into their cave!" (381). To be sure, the aspiring Carol Kennicott, who stands somewhat above the level of the gopher hills honeycombing the Gopher State, is neither cave dweller nor burrowing rodent.

As one might expect, Lewis knowingly in this section makes Carol particularly conscious of her face and figure. Looking through rimless reading glasses, she beholds in her mirror wadded up black hair, bloodless cheeks, thin nose, gentle mouth and chin, "virginal sweetness and timidity" (341). As antidote for having let herself go, she frantically rouges her cheeks, reddens her lips, bares her neck, and assumes the pose of a fandango dancer—only to realize that her heart doesn't dance. It trips later, however, when she makes herself young for the picnic. "Her mirror had asserted that she looked exactly as she had in college, her throat was smooth, her collar-bone not very noticeable" (343). She tells Erik that she is too old to be a nymph, yet thrills to hear him praise her innocent eyes and soft cheeks.

Erik's fascination naturally rekindles Carol's interest in clothes. She commissions the young tailor—without success—to design her a sports suit, and she even deludes herself into seeing her wardrobe as disgraceful: "Everything I have is falling to pieces" (340). Though Will has scheduled a fall trip to Minneapolis, where Carol can buy "new glad-rags" (340), she (out of curiosity and a desire for a hat and blouse) patronizes the millinery of predatory Mrs. Swiftwaite, only to find an unsuitable black-and-red turban, "tabby and small-towny" (341). To become a new woman, so Carol shallowly decides, she must "chuck every stitch" she owns (342). In a self-deprecatory mood, she sees in her mirror a spinsterish mauve hat and a lace-edged modest voile blouse. For the picnic she rejuvenates herself with an adventurous large-bowed sailor blouse, short linen skirt, and white canvas shoes. At home she sits with "a baby-blue book on home-dressmaking" and thinks of Erik (357). On her last bosky walk with him, she acknowledges her rubber overshoes as substitute chaperons. Anxious to flee from Minnesota after Adolph Valborg sneers, "You dirty city women wit' your fine ways and fine dresses!" (385), Carol informs Will that she will wait until California to buy her new clothes.

She never informs Will, however, that in young Erik Valborg she saw something of her father, "the gray reticent judge who was divine love, perfect understanding" (339). So much does she desire this identification that she even overlooks the ex-farmboy's rough hands, so unlike hands she finds attractive, hands as delicate and suave as her resolute father's—and, one might add, Will's, though at this moment infatuated Carol sees in her husband "nothing" of the beloved father-image (339). At three in the morning she awakens and, as decisively as her father on a cruel swindler, pronounces sentence on herself: "A pitiful and tawdry love-affair. No splendor, no defiance. A self-deceived little woman whispering in corners with a pretentious little man" (350). In the hallway nursery, Carol does not think of Will as Hugh's father, for her son's father ought to be someone like Erik, "an older surer Erik" (355). Together the trio would play marvelously inventive games. Clearly Carol has no confidence in Erik's passion.

While the author documents the private gambols of Carol and Erik, he only implies the covert sport of Will and Maud. At any rate, the Kennicotts' new sympathies are patent. Besides sympathizing with Erik's aspirations, Carol empathizes with Fern Mullins's desire to "dance like a hellion" (324). Further, Carol is the only person to comfort and defend the foolish young schoolteacher. Vis-à-vis Erik, Carol at first thinks of herself as hopelessly mature, more advisory even than Vida. Erik is a lamb coaxing Carol to play with him, "because I'm the only one who's decent to him" (342). Too much doth she protest that she is not "in love" with him. When Maud is not flirting with Erik and when Erik is not flirting with everyone, Carol feels tenderness for both. Without a trace of self-mockery she can reflect, "I hate these married women who cheapen themselves and feed on boys" (348). Curiously enough, in Erik's begging eyes she sees the sweet eyes of the little Erdstrom boy.

Thus in seeing in Erik father, husband, and child, Carol plays the psychologically intriguing but confusing roles of daughter, wife, and mother. Although she does not want to hurt Will, her "topsy-turvy honesty" prevents her from making love to him while she is fantasizing about Erik (353); by the same token, she does not want to contaminate her golden dreams of Erik with excitations brought about by Will.

Lewis endows Carol with the wish, the conventional wisdom, that her mind were more masculine—more compartmentalized, capable of keeping sex and love separate. Though she confesses to Will her fondness and admiration for Erik, the young man's appeal to something deep within her, she kisses her husband's hand and promises never to see Erik again. For all Will's literary insensibility, his articulation of Carol's bleak future with the tailor is all too vivid. Her dream of amour is, after all, too weak for *that*.

Between every darkness and herself, Carol now imagines, is her husband, "a bulwark," whom she never really could leave (383). But Carol Kennicott, as bored by humdrum village banalities as Emma Bovary, earlier fantasized about lovers. Galvanized by her first sight of Erik the beautiful stranger, Carol's overwrought imagination has him coming from the Great World. Though hungry for an hour's talk with this Grecian mystery, she ridicules herself as she pictures herself impulsively confiding in him . . . impulsively suggesting that Will invite him to supper. When she learns that her Hellenic herald is none other than "Elizabeth" Valborg, Carol, sickened, envisions the tailor mending a dirty garment and measuring a paunch. But that evening when Uncle Whittier refers to Erik as a milksop show-actor and Aunt Bessie condemns his church manners, Carol sees herself stabbing Uncle with the carving-knife, imagines the headlines, pictures Aunt's gorgeous blood on the tablecloth—then checks herself.

After Carol meets the new schoolteacher—as pretty, well-dressed, flippant, and fond of cities, dancing, parties, and dramatics as herself—she rejoices in the golden dream of *two* new friends. Her romantic foray to the tailor shop with Will's trousers seems suddenly over when Erik acts brusquely, but it revives when, recognizing her by repute, he pays her deference. At his mispronunciation of "pageant," Carol nods kindly, like a lady to a tradesman, while "one of her selves" sneers: "Our Erik is indeed a lost John Keats" (325). Carol, however, comes out of her several conflicting poses to fancy that with Fern and a few others, they might be able to produce a "real play" (325). As Carol rationalizes away Erik's poor grammar, so her imagination, overriding her intellect, pictures him as a bewildered spirit fallen on Gopher Prairie.

Staring later through the rear window of the tailor shop onto the dismal quadrangle of Main Street's chief businesses, she pictures her relationship with the journeyman tailor as a "back-yard romance" (339). It is on the way home that she sees in Erik the beloved father image. As she goes about her chores, Carol imagines herself and some nameless but Erik-like artist building a house in the Berkshires or in Virginia, buying a chair, reading poetry, scrutinizing labor statistics, chatting, walking, picnicking, and playing creative games with an adoring Hugh. Assuming her fandango pose before her mirror, Carol imagines a rose behind one ear, a scarlet mantilla, a bare shoulder. She envisions Erik talking to her kindly, as a father to his child. Finally, Erik's kiss on her *eyelid* wakens her to the reality of her crushing boredom. Still, by night Carol imagines that she *could* submit to some surly, bearded artist of fiction, someone more resolute than Erik. As victim of her vagary, she also imagines her husband dead, maimed, sued, arrested, broken, until only a sudden check of his room dispels her fears. Deeming all Main Street men as leering at her, Carol supposes that Will alone does not know all the truth and all the lies about her romance with Erik.

She feels too reprehensible herself to hinder the flow of Mrs. Bogart's "lustful imagination," her intimation that Fern corrupted Cy in "dark country places" (365). In her room, Carol summons up a "plague of voices" yelping at Fern, with no frontier hero to still the petty scandalmongers (367). Since Gopher Prairie cannot hound a doctor's wife as readily as it can harry a young unmarried schoolteacher, Carol sees Fern as the communal scapegoat. If Carol is not so innocent as she seems, Fern is not so guilty. Still, Lewis has Carol fixing on a symbol out of *The Scarlet Letter,* wondering when the puritanical village will have her on the scaffold. Away from Erik for weeks, she dreams up things he'd say to her, all of which makes her love him more, although at times she is unable to imagine him whole and steady. Groping for decision on her final walk with him, she feels as if she is drifting into a fourth dimension. On the drive back she envisions revealing to Will all her complicated feelings for Erik. Finally, on the snowy December afternoon that she and Will leave Minneapolis for California, the doctor's nervous wife muses on her brief proximity to Erik.

The breach in this section between imagining and thinking widens. In the maundering sermon of the Reverend Zitterel, a restless and bored Carol finds no intellectual exhilaration. So powerful are her first imaginings of Erik's qualities that she checks herself, detecting in his glossiness a hint of the movie actor. After giving herself sound reasons for not going to the tailor shop, she goes anyway. Not until Erik kisses her does the bewildered Carol comprehend that her romance with him is impossible. Still interested in his aspirations, however, she naively seeks a safe friendship. Her tragedy, as she sees it, is to never know tragedy, only farcical complications. Even Fern's disgrace is more hurtful than calamitous, and to make Fern's punishment better fit her crime (of folly, not wickedness), the judge's daughter pressures board member Sam Clark. Lewis has the school board invite Fern, really no longer credible, simply to resign; this seems, under the circumstances, the best move. Lewis also does a sound job of showing Carol's conflicting desires. At times she cannot even picture Erik fully; she sees him as "only an opinion" (375). Is her grand passion, after all, as graceful as she had imagined him?

In this section Carol's psychological and physical exhilaration ride tandem. As she early slips across the lawn to visit Fern Mullins, for example, she is conscious both of Erik and of her dewy feet. Lewis makes her aware of many pleasant little sights and sounds. At the picnic, Carol enjoys swimming and rowing with Erik. On shore and away from the others, he puts his arm around her waist, and she does not resist; but in a fine touch of irony, she is "furious and frightened and exultant by turns" when low-comic Cy later winks at her as a fellow sinner (346). Erik's coming to the Kennicott house the night when Carol is sitting alone on the porch parallels the earlier evening Will goes to the Dyer house when Maud is alone on the porch.

As earlier Carol had led Bresnahan upstairs (with Will) to see Hugh, so now she leads Erik up (without Will). As they lean over the sleeping child, Carol feels, first, Erik's curls against her cheeks and then, in her own room, his reverent kiss. Lewis equates Erik's leaving with the emptiness of the echoing house. On the evening Carol hikes into the country with him, she is aware of her surroundings, especially "the branches dripping, the wet leaves sullenly plumping on the soggy earth" (377), reminding one of the watery images surrounding the delicate metaphor of sea-born Venus in *Madame Bovary*. Lost in the somberness, Carol confesses, "I am happy—so we must go home, before we have time to become unhappy" (377). Like some deus ex machina, Will drives up and rescues the drifting Carol. With Erik's departure from Gopher Prairie, Carol turns to Will, "and for the first time in years they were lovers" (384).

Carol's "Valborg phase" is a masterpiece of insight, self-delusion, and confusion. By calling herself a "neurotic impossibilist," Carol combines Vida's label with a term from her own theory (322). Furthermore, she calls what she is telling herself at age 30 about the 25-year-old Erik "orchard fairy-tales" (322). Her protestations that she is unresponsive to strangers is a splendid bit of self-delusion, but she does sense that her rejoicing in Erik spills over into her rejoicing in village neighborliness. Carol again deludes herself, however, when she insists that her interest is only in helping Erik succeed. In a self-accusing mood, Carol sees herself as a typical small-town woman—modest, moral, safe—the embodiment of the village virus. Still, she convinces herself that she is not really old, just "careless" and "tabby" (342).

Believing that it is too late to love in Erik the "fairy"—that is, the mischievous—she yet feels that she can remake him (355). "You'll be the one thing in which I haven't failed" (356). The irony is more immediate when Carol becomes disgusted with Maud at the picnic—just after Carol convinces herself that she could never become jealous of Maud. Even more ironic, Carol sees Maud playing with Erik, but she never sees her playing with Will. Carol's fondness for Erik, she later tries to persuade herself, is actually her fondness for rebellious youth, for her need "to protest against Things in General" (348). Still, Carol wonders if she really is in love with Erik, if she indeed is unfaithful to Will, if what she wants is, after all, worth the cost. Finally, she decides: "I must get out of this. Quick" (349). Verily, Lewis rejected Cabell's suggestion that Carol commit adultery. As earlier Carol mourned for the day she had walked the queenly battlements, so now she mourns for the clean, quick girl who first came to Gopher Prairie. Beaten with "rods of dullness," she hates the woman she has become—sneaking, tittering, sentimental, jealous, and nervously irresolute (350).

If this self-assessment is sincere, Carol can hardly expect others to admire her; still, when they do, she feels as elated as ever. After she detects in Fern Mullins the "sound of gratitude," Carol becomes even more sympathetic (324). Her maternal air toward Erik ("I'm a thoroughly sound and uninspired schoolma'am") is sheer compliment fishing; but so unaccustomed is she to Erik's "Oh, you aren't *either!*" that she finds it difficult to play "the amused woman of the world" (327). Advising the young man that he does not belong in Gopher Prairie, she imagines his reply: "I've always wanted to know a woman who would talk like that." But to her dismay, Carol hears instead his gaucherie: "Why aren't you happy with your husband?" (331). On the one hand, she urges Erik to become independent; on the other, she feels displeased when he sets up a tennis match "without asking for her inspiration" (333).

Wondering if her "airs" (341) are as laughable as Mrs. Swiftwaite's, Carol recalls: "When I came from the Cities, girls imitated me" (342). At the picnic she detests Maud's sly pleading for Erik's sympathy, but later she herself speaks to him in a "mock-imploring tone" (345). Although Carol is aware—after she and Erik form a mutual admiration society—that her influence on the youth tickles her vanity, she yet asks, self-righteously, if he'd rather become a conformist like Lyman Cass or a rebel like her. She thinks, mistakenly, that only Erik and Hugh need her; and she thinks, also mistakenly, that she would "almost" be content simply to give rather than to receive love (356). A line in Fern's melancholy letter to Carol—"I guess I expected people in Gopher Prairie to admire me"—sums up Carol's own great expectations (374). On their last promenade together, Carol listens not to Erik's words but to his admiring voice; and although his love poetry is as execrable as her nature poetry, Carol nevertheless is its "terribly grateful" recipient (377).

Hypocrisy, as a matter of course, runs rampant in this section. While still peering at Erik after church, Carol takes Will's arm and smiles her devotion to him "in mute assertion" (321). Her newfound panic compels her not only to be attentive to Will, but to equivocate. Finding his intimacies intolerable, she yet longs "to throw into her voice the facile passion of a light woman." She knows that she has become a liar. "I'm snarled with lies and foggy analyses and desires—I who was clear and sure" (353). When Vida questions her about Erik, Carol plays the innocent: "You don't suppose Valborg could actually think about making love to me?" (358). While she sees herself as no "falsely accused innocent" (360), she does see Fern as such and resolves to tell Will "something" about Erik and herself (379). When Adolph Valborg accuses Carol of corrupting his son, she, of course, refutes his falsehood. To protect his wife, Will himself dissembles to Aunt Bessie about Erik's sudden disappearance, indicating that he had advised Erik to find a better job in Minneapolis. And to protect herself, Carol comes up with a pair of fibs—Erik telephoned about his new job and Will needs a vacation—for the benefit of the Jolly Seventeen.

More outré is Carol's wonderment about how many "tombstones of John Keatses" went into making Gopher Prairie's 11 miles of sidewalks (327). Thus she looks at Main Street monotony through Erik's eyes as well as her own. Though she, too, is stirred at times by the sublimity of the broad plains, she rejects the notion that this is "God's Country" and that its future is here and now (331). The back of Main Street is for Carol an objective correlative of her affair with Erik, "an impressionistic picture of dirty grays, drained browns, writhing heaps of refuse" (339). Later the Minniemashie House assaults her sensibilities. Her own house, in fact, is so repellent that she prefers the porch, traditionally the situs of female accessibility.

Though Carol first sees Erik in church, she realizes how many of the good people in Gopher Prairie she does not know. In tune with Will's belief that religion helps control the lower classes, the Reverend Zitterel, always a target for Lewis's barbs, preaches against workers controlling industry. The clergyman corrupts his theological office by sermonizing against women's suffrage in America and a leftist revolution in Russia. In his ludicrous condemnation of Mormonism, the bellicose preacher digresses to blast the unions and the Farmers' Nonpartisan League for killing initiative and enterprise by fixing wages and prices. "There isn't any movement that amounts to a whoop without it's got a moral background" (318). For Zitterel, economics, socialism, and science are simply atheism in disguise. Lewis here prepares the ground for *Elmer Gantry*. In his pre-*Main Street* fiction Lewis presented the West as expansive and the East as restrictive, but Carol sounds like Jack London as she advises Erik to "go East and grow up with the revolution!" (331).

Erik, however, is interested in growing up with Carol, not with the revolution. Through Carol and Erik and through Fern and Cyrus, Lewis dramatizes the fragility of the student-teacher relationship. In this connection, one thinks of Harold Frederic's Celia Madden and Theron in *The Damnation of Theron Ware* (1896) and of Jack London's Ruth Morse and Martin in *Martin Eden* (1909), novels well-known to Lewis. When Carol urges Erik to study Latin without a teacher to make him artificial, the young man declares: "You're my teacher!" (338). While she insists that he look upon her as "a normal wife and good mother," he insists that she *not* look upon him as "a schoolboy" (352). Meanwhile, Fern Mullins foolishly goes to the barn dance with a schoolboy, cynical Cy, her landlady's son. Not only is he one of Fern's imminent students, but he is not much younger than his imminent teacher. When he accuses Fern of inciting him to drink and touch, the school board reacts quickly to Mrs. Bogart's charges that Miss Mullins is too young and inexperienced to teach in the high school. The prudish widow's dirty-minded charge, however, that Fern does ". . . you know what I mean . . ." is in tune with her earlier rumor about the waitress down at Billy's Lunch (366).

That Carol as a judge's daughter shows contempt for the school board's "rules" and "protocol" might strike us as odd, until we recall that her father is in her eyes more an emissary of divine light than a representative of imperfect law. Fearing a permanent stain on Fern's record, Carol entreats Sam Clark to act the frontier hero or at least to turn in a minority report. But because Lewis wants us to like both Fern and Sam, he fuzzes the schoolteacher's error in judgment and the merchant's capacity for heroism. Thus the board, without making charges, simply "accepted" its requested resignation. In the wake of Adolph Valborg's verbal onslaught on Carol, she, too, in a sense, evades a Main Street broadside by resigning with Will from Gopher Prairie for several months.

Erik's boorish father—Lewis's contribution to the agrarian antimyth of the kindly homespun yeoman hero—supposes that before "acting like de animals" his son and the doctor's wife "talk about religion" (385). Half the statement, at least, is true, for Carol has informed Will that Erik does talk about God, "the God that Mrs. Bogart covers up with greasy gingham wrappers" (382). Earlier, when Fern wonders if God is punishing her for ever wanting to drink wine, Carol acknowledges that perhaps the Bogartian god—Main Street's god—is. Too obvious, however, is Lewis's call-to-arms when he has Carol add: "But all the courageous intelligent people are fighting him . . . though he slay us" (369). Whatever else Carol derives from her father's New England, it is not Plymouth Rock's fear of God. Even as a city librarian she felt churchly forces only feebly. Will is one who believes in Christianity without thinking about it, in his church without regularly attending it, and in the dubiousness of Carol's agnosticism without replying to it. The Reverend Zitterel's oblique barb about license in high places is, to Carol, all too transparent.

With the advent of God-conscious, book-conscious Erik Valborg in Gopher Prairie, Carol has a swarm of literary field days. But before she lays interested eyes on the effete pretender, Lewis makes her so appropriately bored in Zitterel's church that she reads the hymnal front matter clear down to the copyright acknowledgments. As Carol and everyone else in town soon learn, "Elizabeth" not only murmurs poetry to Myrtle Cass, but he carts around poetry for show, reminding one of the "very singular deep young man" in Gilbert and Sullivan's *Patience* (1881).

Lewis cleverly foreshadows the essentially literary romance between Carol and Erik by having Will joke about Erik's heavy use of the library. Though nothing ensues, Carol delights in Erik's appeal to her to reestablish a Little Theater. In belletristic conversations with Carol, he bandies about titles, authors, and superficial comments. In her protégé's face, Carol sees Keats, Shelley, and, absurdly enough, Arthur Upson, a poet whom Carol had seen—and young Sinclair Lewis had met—in Minneapolis. Upson's colleagues at the University of Minnesota had published two volumes of his aristocratic verse after his accidental drowning in 1909. A reporter in Waterloo, Iowa, at the time, Lewis wrote a sentimental but sincere editorial-obituary lamenting the death of Upson, whom he exalted as a Keats, a Chatterton, an Adonais.

Carol concludes that Erik, like so many self-made men and women, has read with astonishing breadth and astounding lack of judgment. Still, for all his ardent reading and aspirations, Carol wonders if he is anything but a crude village boy bred on an illiberal farm and in a cheap tailor shop. He tells Carol how, after helping his father clear the fields, he read "this fellow Pater" (331). Adolph Valborg would not joy to hear Carol tell his son that clearing fields is not for him. The notion that broad plains broaden the mind and that high mountains make high purpose Carol sees (as William Dean Howells and Hamlin Garland saw before her) as a favorite American myth. One is relieved to see that Carol's gratitude to Erik for his "Little and tender and merry and wise / With eyes that meet my eyes" is tempered by her literary savoir-faire (377). His instability, Erik informs her, is a result of his leaping from farm to tailorshop to books, from trying to make books alone talk to him.

In line with Carol's view of her life as farce, not tragedy, she feels in the drive back with Will (resembling not in the least the husband in the little Shaw play) like an "unheroic heroine in a drama insanely undramatic" (379). While Will admits to Carol that Erik is "young and likes to gas about books" (381), he touchingly tells her that she is all things he sees in a sunset or country things he likes but can't make poetry of. But when Carol tells Will that Erik has "sensitiveness and talent," Will asks what he's done in "the art line" (382). Lewis foreshadows Erik's "art line," of course, when Carol, on the train to California, turns drearily to illustrations in a screen magazine.

As elsewhere in *Main Street,* Lewis's dreamy illustrations of death take no holiday. One of the disturbing sights Carol observes through the tailorshop rear window is a man in an apron spotted with dry blood, hoisting from a greasy backroom refrigerator a hard slab of meat. Imagining Will dead or dying at one point, Carol rushes to his room, only to retreat after she finds him safe. After the Cy-Fern fiasco, the Reverend Mr. Zitterel reminds Carol that the wages of sin is death—"or anyway, bein' fired" (372). On her last walk in the woods with Erik, flaunting social, not sexual, taboos, Carol convinces herself that if she can't sit and talk with a man by a fire then "I'd better be dead" (378). When threatening Adolph Valborg vents his wrath on her, counterthreatening Carol dares him to tell Will—"and don't blame me when he kills you, when my husband kills you—he will kill you—" (386).

For Carol the territory ahead for the escaping artist, for Erik, is not the new West but the old East. Though earlier she had claimed, thanks to her study of the American small town, that few escapees return, here she asks Erik, "What if you have to go back?" and quickly answers, "Most of us do!" (330). Carol's illogic—Lewis's logic—here foreshadows her own flight and recapture. But on the picnic, Carol, in sailor outfit, finds temporary escape in a rowboat with Erik. Afterward, she rebels against the Widow Bogart's ensnaring questions. In a "passionate escape" (347) there must be a place to flee to, thinks Carol, as well as a place to flee from.[15]

Carol's sudden realization (or rationalization) that her destination is Youth ties in with Quest, Camelot, and the Grail. Ironically, Will (who had advised Maud to get away from Dave for a few days) vetoes his wife's idea of trotting off to Chicago for a few days. That Will has thus thrown her into Erik's arms is now a definite rationalization. "It shows how much I've been longing to escape" (350). Although here she can suppose "any way out," when Erik informs her at the Episcopal lawn-festival that he is going to make her love him, she turns away "with a serene gait that was a disordered flight" (353). Again, when Erik later insists that she does love him, Carol counters: "Can't you understand? Everything crushes in on me so, all the gaping dull people, and I look for a way out—" (356).

Without conviction Carol tells and retells herself that she must not see Erik again, and the sympathetic narrator comments: "She had no ecstatic indulgence in the sense of guilt which is, to the women of Main Street, the surest escape from blank tediousness" (357). Alone in her room, Carol ponders her husband's virtues and bewilderments—his escape into his evening newspaper—and considers ways of leaving him. Carol's departure is practically assured as she imagines herself (and remembers Miles) taking the train. On the drive back from her ramble with Erik, she decides to tell Will about her feelings, to get "out of the trap" (379). When Adolph Valborg later assails her, Carol expresses satisfaction that the son has escaped the father's "muck-heap" (385); but the reticent Lewis has her so shaken by the farmer's "one word"—bitch? whore?—that she wants to flee to California immediately (386). Will, however, prevails upon her not to encourage gossip by their suddenly "running away" (386).

Until scandal falls on her, Carol has no plans, only vague yearnings. The temporary territory ahead for her and Will is, as in the beginning, the West, not the East. Sounding like Will, Carol earlier had told Erik that the prairie future would be magnificent. She adds, however, that he should not be bullied by the present. His future is still in the East. Of course, Will's graphic picture of her future there with Erik, like his earlier interruption of her play watching, brings her suddenly back to reality. Carol foresees that upon her return from California, the young man to whose success she had wanted so much to contribute would be gone from Minneapolis.

10

Passionate Pilgrim

With Erik now out of Carol's life, Lewis in the last six chapters (34 through 39) of *Main Street* details her brief escape from Gopher Prairie with her husband, her dismal return, her eventual and inevitable flight east with her son, and, after Will's romantic visit, her eventual return to Main Street. The April sleet storm that greets the Kennicotts on the day they return to Gopher Prairie from their 14-week tour of the West not only underscores Carol's agitation but effectively forecasts her and Hugh's eventual departure.

Meanwhile, in chapter 35, she nurses the dying Mrs. Perry and abets the broken Champ. Ironically, Major Raymond Wutherspoon, gassed at the Front, returns home a hero. Even with the Commercial Club's "campaign of boosting," the town alters little (397). Finally, after decision, discussion, and preparation, Carol in chapter 36 entrains with her son for the nation's capital—an act that, as the *Dauntless* puts it, "adds another shining star" to Gopher Prairie's service flag (407). Though the war ends a few weeks later, Carol stays on, and in describing her ups and downs in chapter 37, Lewis also maps the pros and cons of capital versus provincial life. In the next chapter emerge figures and ghosts out of Gopher Prairie: Carol entertains the touring Haydocks, discovers that folk hero Bresnahan is a paper tiger in Washington, and that Erik Valborg—Eric Valour—is dismal on the silver screen. When a courtly Will visits his wife in Washington (reminiscent of his courtship visits to St. Paul), Carol warms to him again. After their second honeymoon, in the South, she hints about returning to Gopher Prairie, but Will sagely advises her to wait until she is sure.

Carol eventually comes to see that her conflicting views of Gopher Prairie—one romantic, one naturalistic—are both false. Furthermore, she believes, rightly or wrongly, that she is better able to cope with Main Street. Further still, she is pregnant. Thus after nearly two years in the East, she and Hugh return to the Midwest. Although Carol likes being missed, she realizes in the last chapter that even now Main Street has not really changed. Preoccupied with her baby daughter, she still argues with Will about Hugh's rearing; in the countryside, however, she reclaims old, perhaps deeper, serenities. In the end, Carol Kennicott concedes that Main Street has defeated her. Undaunted by the future, however, she protests that she at least has kept the faith.

Yankee Will Kennicott has also kept the faith, and Lewis's omniscient narrator tells how, thanks to wartime wheat prices, Will and other land speculators with enterprise and horse sense are making money. Noteworthy are the narrator's particulars of Honest Jim Blausser's campaign of boosting. Even in Washington Carol runs into what the narrator describes as a "thick streak of Main Street" (410). He informs us that Carol's progress is "not easy to read" (412). Like Lewis's episodic narrative itself, the chart of Carol's odyssey, the blurred and watery rising and falling lines of her pilgrim's progress, "are broken and uncertain of direction" (413). Whether the omniscient narrator is telling us that Carol, made timid by Main Street, gains from her Washington experience the renewed courage of poise (a kind of interested disinterest) or whether he is telling us that she merely thinks that in this seat of power she has gained this virtue is not clear. Intellectually she seems to understand her false views of Gopher Prairie, but her imagination still tricks her into zigzag emotional recall of the town as either heaven or hell. At one point, the narrator undercuts one of Carol's extremist views—a heavenly one—with the "inside" comment: "She was, perhaps, rather proud of herself for having acquired such tolerance" (425).

But, by and large, Lewis does not satirize his "new woman" in this section of *Main Street.* He does begin, however, by ridiculing the Kennicotts in the Southwest and on the West Coast. Like cartoon tourists, they send 117 postcards back home, and Will spends much travel time palavering about motors, crops, and politics with tourists from 10,000 other Gopher Prairies. Wet from the storm, they wait for a cab at the Haydocks'; with more give than take, Harry spiels about his own California trip; Will, however, manages to get in "one considerable narrative" (390)—a sample of Lowell T. Schmaltz's later monologic tour de force in *The Man Who Knew Coolidge*—about the fellow Minnesotan he met who liked the Kutz Kar "first-rate" (391). Lewis next assaults the crude, red-faced hustler Jim Blausser. His "git-up-and-git" (397) Commercial Club tirade against "knockers" (398) at the pretentious Minniemashie House banquet is a cornucopia of clichés, slang, cuteness, inflation, tastelessness, sentimentality, and bathos—a forecast of Babbitt's celebrated bunk before the Zenith Real Estate Board. Besides pitching into Gopher Prairie's sudden lust for fame and its illusions about its opulent future, Lewis does not neglect to ridicule the dull endeavors of Washington's uncontaminated Tincomb Methodist Church.

Their activities and manners are of a piece with Lewis's earlier cataloging of the Kennicott itinerary and the Minniemashie menu. Lewis's rhetorical listings of Washington sights that delight first Carol and later Will reflect the author's own pleasure from living in Washington during the years he labored over and completed *Main Street.* To be sure, the topics of ardent conversation that Carol hears back in Gopher Prairie are not those she ardently discussed in Washington. The supreme barbershop counsel of Westlake, Hicks, Snaffin, and Clark, after a 15-minute itemized conference on Carol, judges the judge's daughter, all in all, acceptable in Gopher Prairie's sight—and they then move on to the more serious business of new jokes.

Ironically, Carol's remove from Main Street—her moment of truth—is "not the highest in her life, but the lowest and most desolate" (406). As in the paradox of the Fortunate Fall, she now can begin her climb.

Though Washington has no need of Carol's high inspiration, she feels that her bureau work links her, however tenuously, with other world capitals. Lewis skillfully echoes Fort Snelling's sanctified heights when he later places Carol and Will in a moon-enchanted villa balcony above the Charleston Battery. Lewis also allows Carol Kennicott to see what he saw when he made her *Main Street*'s central figure: neither heroic nor melodramatic, her life nevertheless is significant because it articulates the commonplace, the protest of ordinary women.

Back on Main Street, Carol submits to start at the bottom by relieving the restroom attendant an hour a day. Still, she rises to the sublimity of the old Carol when she paints the restroom table a shocking black and orange. Whatever mouse she has labored to bring forth and however defeated she feels in the end, Carol's rhetoric, if nothing else, rises to the level of the proud queen on the ramparts.

About Carol's face and figure in this last section, the author tells us little. His metaphor about small-town tourists in California seeking out citizens from their own states to "stand between them and the shame of naked mountains" (388) is highly ironic—in light of Lewis's early comment (see page 67) that in the Kennicott bedroom Carol undresses behind the closet door. Until the debutantes at the confiserie dissolve Carol's mild sybaritism, she thinks rather well of herself as a smart Washington woman in her black-and-green suit. Back on Main Street in 1920, Carol, now 33 and wearing a fashionable pince-nez, looks forward to more comfortable spectacles, even though they will make her look "older and hopelessly settled" (427). Still, Lewis has Carol projecting her own irrepressible figments—her rebirth in a sense—onto her newborn. Typically enough, she decides not only to send her girl to Vassar but—as if collegiate fashion stood still—to send her off in a tricolette suit and small black hat.

Though Carol loathes Gopher Prairie, she never loses sympathy for certain Gopher Prairieites. Of course, she is "crazy" to see Hugh after the trip west (391), though she quickly finds him spoiled and trying. As she nursed Bea and Olaf, so now she nurses Mrs. Perry; and she solicits a job for Champ as night watchman in Lyman Cass's mill. Although she knows full well that her leaving Gopher Prairie will break Will's heart, she does not commiserate enough with him to stay;

as the train pulls out she feels like jumping off, but she stays aboard. As in St. Paul she had fellow-feeling for her colleagues, so in Washington she has the same for her roommates—one cynical, the other militant. For the visiting Will (whose bewilderments, concealments, and desire for tenderness are as intricate as hers), she develops a firmer respect. Back home she takes her mind off inelegant Main Street by chatting with farmwives and soothing their babies.

Oozing spirit, cramped houses, righteous people—these things Carol's imagination amplified as soon as she had returned from the West. Determined to go east, she cannot help wondering if she will run into Erik there. On the train she imagines that her running away is like a romantic story, but that, unlike a romantic heroine, she is neither doomed nor saved, for her story simply continues. Still, to convince herself that she is mad with joy, she feverishly pictures for Hugh their beyond-the-horizon world of howdahed elephants, rubied maharanees, dove-breasted dawns, and—how like New Englandy Mankato!—a white-and-green house full of books, silver tea sets, and enough cookies to get sick on. At the ripe old age of three and a half, Hugh undercuts his mother's hothouse imagination with "That's foolish" (407).

As a government clerk, Carol fancies the anxiety of men and women awaiting her communiqués. Washington's white columns and parks not only match her earlier imaginings, but, what is more, the woman peering from the upper window of a large dark house provides the daily dose of mystery so lacking in the stale actuality of Gopher Prairie, a town without "secret gates opening upon moors over which one might walk by moss-deadened paths to strange high adventures in an ancient garden" (409). Yet, one recalls, Carol and Hugh did find a path to "high adventure" at the Bjornstams' (305). Besides creating Bovaryesque fantasies, Carol creates imaginary conversations with Will, wherein she defends her Washington friends, her "scoffing enthusiasts" (411).

Her glimpse in Washington of great enterprises, Carol believes, has reduced her exaggerated sense of Main Street's exaggerated importance. Never again, she imagines, will she, thanks to her newfound "poise," project awe onto small-town people (413). After a year in Washington, Carol discovers that office work, more tolerable than housework, is not adventurous; and after the Haydocks leave, Carol nostalgically remembers "lakes and stubble fields . . . the rhythm of insects and the creak of a buggy . . . Sam Clark's 'Well, how's the little lady?' " (415). While working long hours on *Main Street,* Lewis doubtless drew, in part, on the ennui that he felt during the six months in 1910 he spent in Washington as subeditor of the *Volta Review,* a magazine for teachers of the deaf. Carol's sight of Erik in beret and velvet jacket on the screen—the Grail of Youth—prompts her to imagine: "I could have made so much of him—" (416). Although aware of Will's old game of seduction via new prints of Gopher Prairie, Carol cannot help but play once more with the images.

Her decision—"I will go back!" (423)—triggers in her a new romantic myth: in fighting the great tawny prairie beast, her active hate has run out. Romantically, she summons up the hard-working families, the town's awkwardness, its isolated cottages. Through selected images, she sees its lonely solemn people waiting for her to return. Rejoicing in her "fairer attitude" toward the town—"I can love it now!" (425)—she fancies herself running back. But awakening to a nightmare of Ella Stowbody and the Widow Bogart torturing her, she once again realizes that she has mythologized Gopher Prairie into God's Own Country. "We forget so," she tells herself, suddenly seeing the town as altogether vain and uncaring (425). But needing no civet to resweeten her imagination, she fancies (the very next day) a resplendent hometown waiting for her. On the train to Gopher Prairie she feels, in fact, every sensation that she had intensely imagined; but after a week back home she feels neither glad nor sorry.

Her finding little changed on Main Street emerges from reasoned observation, not from her state of mind during Will's visit—again, similar to his St. Paul visits—when she was not so much "analyzing and controlling" events as being swept up by them (418). As Carol ponders her "ordinary" life story, she rightly surmises its significance, though, unlike Sinclair Lewis, she still does not see that her husband's "ordinary" story is also significant (422). To be sure, wearied Carol—who comes to see not people but tyrannical institutions as the enemy—is no superwoman who destroys herself through intellectual overexertion.

Since *Main Street* is Carol Kennicott's story, Lewis describes nothing of Will Kennicott's day-to-day life, nothing of the doctor's apparently robust but convention-preserved affair with Maud Dyer during his wife's absence. Although Carol has male friends in Washington, Lewis offers nothing to suggest that illicit relations are part of her rebellious design. On their trip to the South, the reunited Kennicotts act more like young lovers than a long-married couple. Carol's second pregnancy, in fact, curbs her newfound freedom by drawing the wife and mother back into the ancient institution of family. One is a little disappointed in Lewis's failure to make tattling hay out of Carol's sunny state; surely, *some* Main Streeter, counting back nine months, would have noised abroad at least *one* consequence of Will's visit east.

On her hunting excursion with the Clarks, Will's glorious playmate—stalking ducks instead of culture—learns to shoot a shotgun. On the bank of a reedy lake, she listens restfully to Ethel Clark drawling about nothing in particular, and she listens to the men's voices rising above the freshly plowed fields in the still dusk. To the texture of Carol's aesthetic pleasure here Lewis has the renewed progenitress become conscious on the drive back to town of "an unbroken sweep of land to the Rockies, to Alaska" (431). This scene effectively turns the narrative back to the first hilltop scene, the breeze crossing a thousand miles of fertile wheat land and, in retrospect, bellying the skirt of a rebellious girl, "the spirit of that bewildered empire called the American Middlewest" (8).

Before Carol had departed for Washington to discover the "greatness of life"—the search for being—she had informed Will that she might come back to Gopher Prairie if she could return with "something more than I have now" (405). Presumably the "something more" is not another child but "poise"—defined as "amiable contempt" and "unembittered laughter" (413). Oddly, however, the government clerk's intensified poise seems to have deserted her in the intimidating vicinity of the four clattering jazz age debs, clearly Fitzgeraldian baby vamps who banter in cafés and kiss in the dark. One assumes that although Carol is glad of her rebellion, of her moral victory, a more mature, more tolerant doctor's wife will return to Gopher Prairie. The narrator tells us that in spite of her wounded vanity, Carol manages to laugh at herself for expecting to be welcomed home as both heretic and hero. To her long list of Gopher Prairie defeats she adds Community Day. Though skeptical of her own abilities, Carol does not mock her ideals and failures. By allowing Carol to pass on the challenge, to hope for success in the next generation, Lewis broadcasts his own faith in progress.

Like Lewis at Yale, Carol in Washington yearns for "some special learning." Oddly and unfortunately, she wants this learning not for soul saving (as she had claimed back in Gopher Prairie) but rather as a means to "distinguish" herself in others' eyes (411). Although pointing out people and places to the visiting Haydocks soothes her vanity, Carol realizes that nobody in Washington really frets about her. Her thirst for admiration remains unquenched. As a Washington insider she savors the impression that she makes on her own husband. Back on Main Street Carol is "excited by each familiar and hearty greeting, and she is flattered to be, for a day, the most important news in the community" (425). Though Vida looks for "imported heresies" (426), a bubbling Juanita now takes Carol to her "social bosom" (425). Champ Perry squeaks: "We all missed you terrible." Lewis enhances Carol's refrain—"Who in Washington would miss her?"—by his reliable stratagem of not granting names to Carol's Washington circle (426). Sadly, however, few in Gopher Prairie ask her for facts about Washington the way many would beg opinions from Bresnahan. Characteristically, Maud Dyer—resenting the wife's return—sounds her out about Washington men.

On the Kennicotts' return from California, Carol had thought, "I'm out of practice in lying" (392). Unlike Will, she embarrassingly balks at greeting Sam Clark in the jocund country custom. Knowing that she will quit Gopher Prairie, she still answers "Yes" to Will's "Pretty good to be back, eh?" (394)—another example of her much earlier seen "self-protective maturity" (41). She finds Blausser's flimflam and the publicity booklet with its chaff about Gopher Prairie's culture, comfort, and world-famous lakes especially offensive. Dissatisfied and rankled, Carol rationalizes her impending leave-taking as an act committed for Will's sake.

In a freshly painted garage, a new chicken fence, and a new sign on Main Street Carol finds none of her husband's joy, only the frozen decay of "scarecrows in a shanty town" (392). What she sees is a far cry from Blausser's big city apparition of Gopher Prairie, a town already as refined and cultured as "any burg on the whole bloomin' expanse of God's Green Footstool" (400). Besides the promotion tract booklet (which prompts Carol to comment ironically, "*There's* where I want to go"), the key elements in the "Watch Gopher Prairie Grow" campaign (toward factories and state institutions) are a baseball team, a few blocks of bright electric lights, and—one thinks today of Meredith Wilson's River City in *The Music Man*—a uniformed band (401). The retired farmers move onto the more expensive town lots, but Carol sees no cultural improvement, only more egomaniacalism. If she found pockets of Main Street even in Washington, she also found there pockets of arcana not of Main Street. And although she learned of towns in America worse than Gopher Prairie, Carol still does not admit that Main Street is "as beautiful as it should be . . . that Gopher Prairie is greater or more generous than Europe!" (432).

On her first day back from California, Carol listens to the old Kennicott house reeking with "colorless stillness" (393). Then comes the expected—Will's eternal basement sounds: removing the ashes, shoveling the coal. No longer able to endure the house, Carol rushes down to the large clean basement. There Will, whistling tenderly, stares at the glowing furnace, at the "black-domed monster," *his* "symbol of home," of "beloved routine," of "pure bliss" (394). Interestingly, Richard Wright—who cited *Main Street* as the first novel he devoured—turned this glowing symbol of home into a symbol of black rage in *Native Son* (1940), a novel that Lewis, in turn, praised highly. Surely Lewis nods when he has his furnace-loving Kennicott promise Carol in Washington that, except for the garage and plumbing, he will build the new house to suit her. Poignantly, he also confesses that during his wife's absence he did not open the summer cottage and that, not wanting to go into the still and empty house, he sat late into the night on the front porch—another nice touch of Lewisian role-reversal.

To Lewis's credit, Carol undergoes no miraculous change. The logic of her characterization is consistent from start to finish. What

Carol thinks she acquires in the nation's capital, as we noted, is an impersonal attitude toward Gopher Prairie that Gopher Prairie itself lacks. Will's first bit of back-home news on his Washington visit is the excavation for the new school building. Indeed, Vida's triumph stirs the returned Carol to humble activities. As earlier she had imagined Yale or Oxford for her son, so now, despite her education in disillusionment, she fancies Vassar for her daughter. Will, in fact, thinks that Hugh should "start getting educated" now, "learn a little discipline" (430). Reflecting the advanced thinking of the day that society would be better if children were reared with permissive understanding, Carol declares that she has learned more discipline and education from him than he has learned from her, which causes Will to mock his wife's "new-fangled ideas" about child rearing (430). With no mention of educator Maria Montessori (1870-1952), Carol asserts that her biggest job now is to allow Hugh to develop his thoughts in his own way and to keep his parents from "educating" him (430)—and, the reader might add, to keep Mom from choosing his college.

No sooner does Carol think that she has left behind, among other things, that old-time, small-town religion than Lewis manages a bit of supreme but convincing irony. On the train, Hugh announces that he delights not only in Auntie Bogart's cookies but also in her talks—as no doubt Cy did not—about the Dear Lord. Why, he wonders, does his mother never talk to him about the Dear Lord, especially since, as Auntie Bogart says, he is going to be a preacher? Carol can only beg her lamb to wait until her generation has stopped rebelling before his begins. No spurner of all social convention, Carol, thanks to Vida's letters, first becomes acquainted with the "nicer" members of Washington's Tincomb Methodist Church. Here she finds, as she found in California, a "transplanted and guarded" Main Street (409), with two-thirds of the congregation hailing from small towns. She finds the church suppers in Washington dull. Back in Gopher Prairie, she feels once more the force of village religiosity when she learns that Prohibition is Ma Bogart's latest cause, with Sabbatarianism in the offing.

As in California quixotic Carol lived for a few moments in a "romantic novel" simply by chatting with a painter on a foggy dune (388), so in Washington she discerns a "mystery, a romance, a story" simply by looking up at a woman peering through a window of a dark house (409). Are we to intuit that this woman in Washington is as lonely as Carol was in Gopher Prairie? To be sure, Carol Kennicott's entrée into the Washington wonderland calls up Bea Sorenson's in megalopolitan Gopher Prairie. Certain men in Washington remind Carol of fictional explorers and aviators, a real-life breed that Lewis himself read about, wrote about, and duly admired. And the stimulating "talking, talking, talking" in Carol's shared apartment is not, oddly enough, the artist-studio talk of fiction but the sober talk of office workers who think in terms of cataloging and statistics. But even in the rousing capital, Carol relishes her "motionless evenings of reading" (411).

Still, for the sake of his plot, Lewis must place her one day in a motion-picture house to view an abysmal photodrama about—what else?—decadent studio-artists. To underscore the artificiality of languishing Eric Valour playing a dummy piano in a canvas room, Lewis nimbly shows Carol in the next scene back in her apartment. As if in some final rite of Erik-exorcism, she rereads Will's letters—stiff, sketchy, but *very real.*

Will's little blandishment on his Washington visit (that back in Gopher Prairie Carol will have Sam Clark and him "reading poetry and everything") is unlikely, but it does point to Carol's eventual return (420). By having his central character wonder about her own life as "story"—a tale without heroics, melodrama, magic—Lewis conveys the value of his own theme—the protest, as we earlier noted, of the ordinary. And by articulating Carol's commonplace intricacy, he also implies Will's. Ironically, Lewis's quartet of barbershop critics harmonizing on the return of Doc's wife gives her a "pass," concluding that the friendship between Carol Kennicott and Erik Valborg was *strictly* literary "and all that junk" (428). Finally, to show both her new accommodation to Main Street *and* "the tragedy of struggle against inertia," Lewis has Carol acquiescing to the village virus, to see what Ethel Clark promises will be an "awful exciting" movie—this instead of reading the book that Carol had planned to read (431).

Another spur to Carol's earlier farewell to Main Street is the raucous campaign of boosting. Like the Reverend Zitterel earlier, Jim

Blausser blasts all knockers of prosperity and property, particularly the Farmers' Nonpartisan League and the "whole bunch of socialists" (399). Terrifying to Carol is the knowledge that Wakamin businessmen, led by their sheriff, rode a "pro-German" league organizer out of town on a rail (403). The reason, Carol concludes, is economics, not sedition. Lewis's choice of Wakamin distances the disgrace from Gopher Prairie but intimates that "it can happen here." In Washington, she hears more horror stories about American towns, of heresy hunts in the wake of labor-management clashes. In Washington Carol had joined a union, gone on strike, felt personal solidarity, and expressed brave thoughts, but since she has no hard-driving ambition her use to dedicated radicals there is limited.

Fresh from her absolution of guilt by the "generalissima of suffrage" and by her discussions about revolution and socialism (422), she wonders if her baby daughter will see "an industrial union of the whole world" (432). Lewis ends Carol's story so close to the 1920 publication date of *Main Street* that he himself could not know then that "revolution" would not be the buzz word during the Roaring Twenties that it had been during the Progressive Era and would become again during the Great Depression. Though Lewis found personal excitement and literary material in his own early Bohemianism and Leftist exhibitionism, political movements as such were never his chief concern.

Lewis's death images in this last section ultimately give way to images of life. On her return from the West Carol had noticed black branches, decayed snow, tall dead weeds in vacant lots, ash heaps, and dog-bones. Only her son, Carol believes, is holding her to Gopher Prairie, for "If Hugh died—" (394). While trying to readjust to the new tedium, Carol is not touched as personally by the war as is Vida, who raves about the need to invade Germany and to massacre German men, for German soldiers crucify prisoners and cut off babies' hands. From his biting attack on Vida's propaganda Lewis turns to Mrs. Perry's death by pneumonia and the sentimentality of her shabby funeral and Champ's lying on the snowy mound. Square-jawed, erstwhile hennish Raymie returns home a seasoned infantry officer with apparently no trauma from the blood and mud and gas of trench warfare; Will politely asks the muscular Christian the meaning of "Going West" (396). Finding work in Washington with the Bureau of War Risk Insurance (a forerunner of the Veterans Bureau and Veterans Administration), Carol, like Una Golden in *The Job* (1917), is disillusioned by her discovery that afternoon office routine "stretches to the grave" (408). Erik on the screen suggests sterility and Will in his letters life. By the time she leaves Washington, *life* indeed is stirring in Carol.

The "campaign of boosting" is designed to overcome inertia, to create prosperity for the townspeople. Overcoming her own inertia—the crisis in *Main Street*—Carol leaves Gopher Prairie. When she returns nearly two years later she fancies that all the world is changing. But the hot topics in Gopher Prairie are prohibition, the high cost of living, the presidential election, the Clarks' new car, and the foibles of Cy Bogart. Over the seven new bungalows and two garages Carol cannot rhapsodize, but in the new school she sees hope. In the inevitable humdrum struggles against inertia she sees the only tragedy.

Her earlier jaunts to and from Minneapolis and Joralemon and California foreshadow her journey to and from Washington. Even on the trip west Carol is restless, dodging her thoughts, hiding her doubts, persuading herself that she is tranquil. She commits the fallacy of elsewhere—"of running away . . . of moving on to a new place" (389)—familiar to the vagabond Lewis. Feeling after the trip that she has never been away, knowing that she must leave again, Carol bides her time. Another rationalization that Carol devises for her leave-taking is that if Gopher Prairie is as beautiful as Blausser, the *Dauntless*, and the Commercial Club proclaim, then her work is over and "she could go" (401).

Unlike Ibsen's Nora Helmer, who escapes from husband and children forever (and slams the Doll House door), Lewis's Carol Kennicott escapes from Will only temporarily, takes her son with her, and does not slam the door. Her daydreams of someday taking a train somewhere, however, do come true. She is akin to a pilgrim passionately fleeing from parochial persecution, and Will's dictum about nobody solving a problem by "running away from it" requires new definition: "I'm going to be quiet and think. I'm going! I have a right to my own life" (405). In light of Lewis's making so little of the

Kennicott-Milford wedding, Carol's modernistic separation hardly seems profane. In terms of Gopher Prairie's failures, however, her exodus repeats the departures of Miles, Fern, and Erik.

In the crowded capital Carol finally talks with "other Carols," but she also overhears women younger and bolder than herself smoking and chattering about "running up to New York" for some racy theater (414). Ironically, she who quested for youth, now feeling herself old, rustic, and plain (as she had felt just before her romance with Erik), is consumed by the desire to flee from these "hard brilliant children to a life easier and more sympathetic" (414). Although most people fleeing small towns stay in the city, Carol reinforces the older Friendship Village tradition (but not the "happy ending" tradition) by returning to Main Street.

And she is recaptured without even Major Wutherspoon's mite of glory. Unlike the expatriates fleeing to Paris, she gives herself only the vaguest of self-promises about someday visiting Europe. Carol's return to Gopher Prairie is not unlike Lewis's return to Yale after his cattle-boat trip to Liverpool. As he could reject or take the institution on more realistic terms, so Carol, one might suppose, could brood less over what the country town could *not* give. Still, one recalls that in *Dodsworth* insistent Mrs. Fern Dodsworth, Carol's older, more selfish, more pretentious counterpart, runs off—to no avail—with a young but poor Austrian nobleman.

To sustain herself in facing the future, Carol enjoys the generalissima's homework orders. Maybe civilization will come in only 20,000 years (not in 200,000) if enough housewives ask people to define their jobs. The question is interesting and important, of course, although one remains skeptical of the generalissima's clairvoyance. The questions that Carol dreams up, at any rate, are merely silly. In spite of her best efforts, Carol in Washington still shelters an ambivalent naturalistic-romantic view of Gopher Prairie. Never will she be truly superior to her environment. On the drive back to town after Carol's hunting trip with Will and the Clarks, Lewis makes Carol conscious of the vast sweep of land that "will rise to unexampled greatness when other empires have grown senile." But to underscore Carol's surmise that before that time a long line of aspiring women ("a hundred generations of Carols") will go down in forgetful defeat in the struggle against inertia, the author has her charitably accede to Ethel Clark's invitation to see a trivial flick (431).

In the problem's complexity, in its mix of disappointment and hope, Lewis exhibits what back then was labeled the "new realism." Though defeated by Main Street's heavy hand, Carol as quasi-quester now points to her sleeping daughter, "a bomb," she informs Will, "to blow up smugness." As a sleepy Will prepares for the future (by winding the clock) Carol invites him to imagine "what that baby will see and meddle with before she dies in the year 2000!" (432). To be sure, Carol's Wellsian prophecies about global industrialization and "aeroplanes" to Mars seem not so farfetched today. But concerned more with tomorrow than with 30,000 tomorrows, a yawning Will rummages around for next day's collar, senses snowfall, and sensibly thinks about putting up the storm windows.

The immediacy, the reality, of *his* vision prompts him to speak those utterly practical words with which Sinclair Lewis brings *Main Street,* in its moment of final suspense, to a perfectly commonplace close: "Say," Will asks his farseeing wife, "did you notice whether the girl put that screw-driver back?" (432). His allusion to "the girl" distances the latest Kennicott maid while foregrounding his highly utilitarian household question—as well as its implied question as to whether his highly idealistic helpmate is also, in truth, "back."

Notes

1. See Theodore Spencer, "The Critic's Function," *Sewanee Review* 47 (October–December 1939): 556. When asked what he thought of tracing his work to the French realists, Lewis paradoxically replied: "Nothing. The only source for *Main Street* that I am aware of was Malory's *Morte D'Arthur;* I wrote *Main Street* because there was nothing like Malory in the Middle West."

2. Sinclair Lewis, "Introduction to *Main Street,*" in *The Man from Main Street,* ed. Harry E. Maule and Melville Cane (New York: Random House, 1953), 214.

3. Mark Schorer, *Sinclair Lewis: An American Life* (New York: McGraw-Hill Book Co., 1961), 102; hereafter cited in text.

4. Sinclair Lewis, in *From Main Street to Stockholm,* ed. Harrison Smith (New York: Harcourt, Brace and Co., 1952), 20.

5. Lewis, "How I Wrote a Novel on Trains and beside the Kitchen Sink," in *The Man from Main Street,* 201–2.

6. Mark Schorer, *Sinclair Lewis: A Collection of Critical Essays* (Englewood Cliffs, N. J.: Prentice-Hall, 1962), 8.

7. John F. McCarthy, "A New Look at an Old Street," *English Journal* 57 (October 1968): 987.

8. Vernon Parrington, "Sinclair Lewis: Our Own Diogenes," in *Main Currents in American Thought,* vol. 3 (New York: Harcourt, Brace and Co., 1927), 365. Diogenes, the Cynic, an ancient Greek philosopher, exhibited contempt for life's amenities.

9. Meredith Nicholson, "Let Main Street Alone," in *The Man in the Street* (New York: Charles Scribner's Sons, 1921), 8.

10. Sinclair Lewis, introduction to David L. Cohn, *The Good Old Days* (New York: Simon and Schuster, 1940), viii.

11. Sinclair Lewis, *Cass Timberlane* (New York: Random House, 1946), 288.

12. William B. Yeats, "The Land of Heart's Desire," in *The Poetical Works: Dramatic Poems*, vol. 2 (New York: Macmillan Co., 1907), 151.

13. Lord Dunsany, "The Laughter of the Gods," in *Plays of God and Men* (New York: G. P. Putnam & Sons, 1923), 63.

14. John Henry Newman, *The Idea of a University* (Oxford: Clarendon Press, 1976), 128.

15. In *The Escape Motif in the American Novel: Mark Twain to Richard Wright* (Columbus: Ohio State University Press, 1972), Sam Goldfarb does not treat *Main Street,* but he quotes this idea from the novel as the motto of his study.

Selected Bibliography

Primary Works

Hike and the Aeroplane. New York: Stokes, 1912 (pseud. Tom Graham).

Our Mr. Wrenn: The Romantic Adventures of a Gentle Man. New York: Harper, 1914.

The Trail of the Hawk: A Comedy of the Seriousness of Life. New York: Harper, 1915.

The Job: An American Novel. New York: Harper, 1917.

The Innocents: A Story for Lovers. New York: Harper, 1917.

Free Air. New York: Harcourt, Brace and Howe, 1919.

Main Street: The Story of Carol Kennicott. New York: Harcourt, Brace and Howe, 1920.

Babbitt. New York: Harcourt, Brace, 1922.

Arrowsmith. New York: Harcourt, Brace, 1925.

Mantrap. New York: Harcourt, Brace, 1926.

Elmer Gantry. New York: Harcourt, Brace, 1927.

The Man Who Knew Coolidge: Being the Soul of Lowell Schmaltz, Constructive and Nordic Citizen. New York: Harcourt, Brace, 1928.

Dodsworth. New York: Harcourt, Brace, 1929.

Ann Vickers. Garden City, N.Y.: Doubleday, Doran, 1933.

Work of Art. Garden City, N.Y.: Doubleday, Doran, 1934.

Selected Short Stories. Garden City, N.Y.: Doubleday, Doran, 1935.

It Can't Happen Here. Garden City, N.Y.: Doubleday, Doran, 1935.

The Prodigal Parents. Garden City, N.Y.: Doubleday, Doran, 1938.

Bethel Merriday. Garden City, N.Y.: Doubleday, Doran, 1940.

Gideon Planish. New York: Random House, 1943.

Cass Timberlane. New York: Random House, 1946.

Kingsblood Royal. New York: Random House, 1947.

The God-Seeker. New York: Random House, 1949.

World So Wide. New York: Random House, 1951.

From Main Street to Stockholm: Letters of Sinclair Lewis, 1919–1930. Selected and introduced by Harrison Smith. New York: Harcourt, Brace, 1952.

The Man from Main Street: A Sinclair Lewis Reader. Selected Essays and Other Writings, 1904–1950. Edited by Harry E. Maule and Melville H. Cane. New York: Random House, 1953.

I'm a Stranger Here Myself, and Other Stories. Selected and introduced by Mark Schorer. New York: Dell, 1962.

The Sinclair Lewis Papers are at Yale University, with a sizable collection (including the manuscripts of *Main Street*) at the University of Texas at Austin, and a fine collection of Lewis's books and other publications at Macalester College, St. Paul.

Secondary Works

Books and Parts of Books

Aaron, Daniel. "Sinclair Lewis, *Main Street.*" In *The American Novel,* edited by Wallace Stegner, 166–79. New York: Basic Books, 1965. Influences on *Main Street* and its historical importance.

Blake, Nelson Manfred. "Knockers and Boosters: Sinclair Lewis." In *Novelist's America: Fiction as History 1910–1940.* Syracuse, N.Y.: University of Syracuse Press, 1969. Realistic elements in *Main Street.*

Bloom, Harold, ed. *Sinclair Lewis.* Modern Critical Views. New York: Chelsea House, 1987. Reprints 10 essays, including Nan Bauer Maglin's "Women in Three Sinclair Lewis Novels."

Bucco, Martin, ed. *Critical Essays on Sinclair Lewis.* Boston: G. K. Hall & Co., 1986. Contains an extensive introduction to Lewis's critical reception, reprints Mencken's review of *Main Street,* Flanagan's "A Long Way to Gopher Prairie," and Light's "The Quixotic Motif in *Main Street,* with Lundquist's original "The Sauk Centre Sinclair Lewis Didn't Write About."

_____. "Main Street." In *Reference Guide to American Literature,* edited by D. L. Kirkpatrick, 656–57. Chicago and London: St. James Press, 1987. Highlights novel's form and function.

_____. "Sinclair Lewis Centennial Conference." In *Dictionary of Literary Biography Yearbook: 1985,* edited by Jean W. Ross, 145–47. Detroit: Gale Research Co., 1986. Report of anniversary activities in St. Cloud and Sauk Centre.

Connaughton, Michael, ed. *Sinclair Lewis at 100: Papers Presented at a Centennial Conference.* St. Cloud, Minn.: St. Cloud State University, 1985. Contains 24 papers, 6 treating *Main Street.*

Dooley, D. J. *The Art of Sinclair Lewis.* Lincoln: University of Nebraska Press, 1967. Discusses in *Main Street* and in other novels the relationship between Lewis's artistic weakness and his raising important social questions.

Fleming, Robert E., with Esther Fleming. *Sinclair Lewis: A Reference Guide.* Boston: G. K. Hall & Co., 1980. Indispensable bibliography of reviews, articles, and books on Lewis and his work, with scores of items on *Main Street.*

Grebstein, Sheldon. *Sinclair Lewis.* New York: Twayne, 1962. Compact overview of Lewis's works praises *Main Street* for breaking through public hostility toward unpleasant novels.

Herron, Ima H. "Crusaders and Skeptics." In *The Small Town in American Literature,* 334–428. Durham, N. C.: Duke University Press, 1939. Relates *Main Street* and other Lewis novels to the tradition of the village novel.

Hilfer, Anthony Channell. "Sinclair Lewis: Caricaturist of the Village Mind." In *The Revolt from the Village: 1915–1930,* 158–92. Chapel Hill: University of North Carolina Press, 1969. Discusses the sociological form and content of Lewis's attack on the small town.

Holman, C. Hugh. "Anodyne for the Village Virus." In *The Comic Imagination in American Literature,* edited by Louis D. Rubin, Jr., 247–58. New Brunswick, N.J.: Rutgers University Press, 1973. Describes Lewis's satiric methods in *Main Street.*

Lewis, Grace Hegger. *Half a Loaf.* New York: Horace Liveright, 1931. Novel of her marriage to Lewis, who as the character Timothy Hale writes a popular novel called *God's Own Country.*

_____. *With Love from Gracie: Sinclair Lewis, 1912–1925.* New York: Harcourt, Brace, 1955. Nonfiction version of *Half a Loaf* depicts Lewis at work on *Main Street.*

Light, Martin. *The Quixotic Vision of Sinclair Lewis.* West Lafayette, Ind.: Purdue University Press, 1975. Sees Lewis as transferring to Carol Kennicott and other central characters his own quixotism.

Lundquist, James. *Sinclair Lewis.* Literature and Life Series. New York: Frederick Ungar Publishing Co., 1973. Discusses the relationship between American mass culture and "pop" aspects of Lewis's art.

Schorer, Mark. *Sinclair Lewis: An American Life.* New York: McGraw-Hill Book Co., 1961. Official massive, urbane, critical biography is an essential source for information on Lewis and his work. Contains useful checklist of Lewis's writings.

———, ed. *Sinclair Lewis: A Collection of Critical Essays.* Twentieth Century Views. Englewood Cliffs, N.J.: Prentice-Hall, 1962. Contains best evaluations of Lewis's work before 1960.

———. Afterword to *Main Street.* Signet Classic, 433–39. New York: New American Library, 1961. Describes novel in terms of its historical value.

Turim, Maureen. "I Married a Doctor: Main Street Meets Hollywood." In *The Classic American Novel and the Movies,* edited by Gerald Peary and Roger Shatzkin, 206–17. Frederick Ungar Publishing Co., 1977. Describes alterations from book to film.

Tuttleton, James W. "Sinclair Lewis: The Romantic Comedian as Realist Mimic." In *The Novel of Manners in America,* 141–61. Chapel Hill: University of North Carolina Press, 1972. Lewis's defense of the small town in early novels turns to attack in *Main Street.*

Wells, Carolyn. *Ptomaine Street: The Tale of Warble Petticoat.* Philadelphia and London: J. B. Lippincott, 1921. Parody of *Main Street* in both form and format.

Journal Articles

Flanagan, John T. "The Minnesota Backgrounds of Sinclair Lewis's Fiction." *Minnesota History* 37 (March 1960): 1–13. Treats the backgrounds from which Lewis created Gopher Prairie and his other fictional communities.

Gurko, Leo and Miriam. "The Two Main Streets of Sinclair Lewis." *College English* 4 (February 1943): 288–92. Focuses on Lewis's satiric ambivalence in *Main Street.*

Lewis, Grace Hegger. "When I Walked Down Main Street." *New York Times Magazine,* 3 July 1960, 28–29. Recalls her first momentous visit to Sauk Centre.

Lundquist, James, ed. *Sinclair Lewis Newsletter.* 8 vols. 1969–76. Contains articles on *Main Street* dealing with revisions, its influences, Carol's characterization, and its value in the classroom.

Thompson, Dorothy. "The Boy and Man from Sauk Centre." *Atlantic Monthly* 206 (November 1960): 39–48. Lewis's second wife recalls the novelist's ambivalence toward his family and his hometown.

Van Doren, Carl. "The Revolt from the Village: 1920." *Nation* 113 (12 October 1921): 407–12. Speculates on influence of Edgar Lee Masters's *Spoon River Anthology* on Lewis, Sherwood Anderson, Zona Gale, and Floyd Dell.

Index

Ade, George, 33
The Adventures of Huckleberry Finn (Twain), 3
The Age of Innocence (Wharton), 14, 15
American Literature and Social Change (Spindler), 19
"The American Village" (Freneau), 5
Anderson, Margaret, 16
Anderson, Sherwood, 5, 13, 15, 82, 83, 93, 94
Androcles and the Lion (Shaw), 65, 74
Ann Vickers (Lewis), 7
Anna Karénina (Tolstoy), 5
The Apprenticeship of Wilhelm Meister (Goethe), 81
Arnold, Matthew, 60
Arrowsmith (Lewis), 6, 9
The Art of Sinclair Lewis (Dooley), 19
Arthur, King, 4
Austen, Jane, 13, 60
Babbitt (Lewis), 6, 9, 16
Babbitt, George F. (fictional), 116
Balzac, Honoré de, 4, 41, 42–43
Bechhofer, C. H., 16
Beck, Warren, 17
Bethel Merriday (Lewis), 7
Bierce, Ambrose, 70
Bjornstam, Bea (fictional), 26, 33, 50, 51, 52, 53, 55, 61, 64, 72, 76, 79, 80, 81, 86, 90, 92, 93, 94, 96, 100, 117, 124
Bjornstam, Miles (fictional), 48–49, 50, 51, 52, 54, 55, 57, 60, 61, 62, 64, 70, 72, 76, 79–80, 81, 86, 91, 93, 95, 96, 100, 112, 127
Bjornstam, Olaf (fictional), 80, 81, 86, 90, 94, 117
Bjornstam family (fictional), 80, 86, 88, 118
Blausser, Jim (fictional), 6, 115, 116, 121, 122, 124–25, 126

Blodgett College (fictional), 29, 31, 32, 34, 40, 41, 45, 52, 58, 70, 80
Bloom, Harold, 21
Bloom, Molly (fictional), 69, 90
Bogart, Cyrus N. (fictional), 48, 51, 54, 56, 62, 66, 71, 85, 87, 98, 99, 100, 104, 105, 109, 111, 123, 126
Bogart, Mrs. (fictional), 27, 28, 41, 64, 67, 69, 74, 80, 83, 88, 99, 104, 109, 110, 112, 119, 123
A Book of Prefaces (Mencken), 93
Bovary, Emma (fictional), 67, 82, 88, 98, 103, 118
Bresnahan, Percy (fictional), 85, 87, 88, 89, 90, 91, 93, 95, 97, 105, 114–15, 121
Brieux, Eugène, 41
Bright Metal (Stribling), 20
Brown, Sir Thomas, 42
Browning, Robert, 60, 72
Bruin, Maire (fictional), 73
Bucco, Martin, 20–21
Burns, Robert, 60
Byron, George Gordon, Lord, 60

Cabell, James Branch, 15, 16, 77, 95, 106
Calabree, Dr. and Mrs. (fictional), 89
California, 48, 99, 101, 104, 115, 116, 117, 121, 122, 123, 126
Calverton, V. F., 17
Camelot (fictional), 4, 37, 38, 44, 59, 112
Canby, Henry Seidel, 17
Cane, Melville H., 18, 129n2
Canfield, Dorothy, 14
Carlyle, Thomas, 41
Carmen (Bizet), 29
Carolyx (fictional), 73
Carroll, Lewis, 34
Cass, Lyman (fictional), 57, 60, 61, 69, 81, 107, 117
Cass, Myrtle (fictional), 99, 110
Cass family, (fictional), 50
Cass Timberlane (Lewis), 7, 58, 129n11
Catalogs, 29–30, 50, 65–66, 86, 93, 100, 116
Cather, Willa, 5, 34
Cedar, Allan (fictional), 58
Charming, Prince (fictional), 69, 74
Chatauqua, 76, 77, 78, 81, 82, 83
Chatterton, Thomas, 111
Chicago, 26, 28, 29, 34, 41, 112
Clark, Ethel (fictional), 27, 35, 39, 94, 120, 124, 128
Clark, Sam (fictional), 27, 35, 36, 37, 42, 69, 92, 105, 109, 116, 119, 124
Clark family (fictional), 30, 32, 33, 34, 44, 45, 56, 120, 126, 127
Cleveland, Grover, 2
Cohn, David L., 30, 129n10
Conrad, Joseph, 58, 59
Cooper, James Fenimore, 78
Crane, Helga (fictional), 20
Crane, Stephen, 4
Critical Essays on Sinclair Lewis (ed. Bucco), 21

Daggett, Milt (fictional), 43
The Damnation of Theron Ware (Frederic), 14, 42, 94, 109
Darwin, Charles, 40
Dashaway, Chester (fictional), 42, 44
Dauntless (fictional), 27–29, 65, 70, 114, 126
"Dauphin" (fictional), 29
Dawson, Luke (fictional), 48, 49
Dawson, Mrs. (fictional), 48, 58
Dawson family (fictional), 50
Death, 37, 44–45, 61–62, 72, 74, 75, 89, 95–96, 104, 111–12, 125–26
Defoe, Daniel, 17
Dell, Floyd, 94

De Quincey, Thomas, 60
DeVoto, Bernard, 17
Dialogue, 10, 13–14, 27, 28, 29, 71
Dickens, Charles, 4, 17, 42, 60, 96
Dillon, Dr. Harvey (fictional), 68
Dillon, Mrs. (fictional), 66–67
Ditte (Nexö), 93
The Divine Comedy (Dante), 81
Dodsworth (Lewis), 6, 9, 127
Dodsworth, Fern (fictional), 127
Dodsworth, Sam (fictional), 6
A Doll's House (Ibsen), 126
Don Quixote (Cervantes), 8
Dooley, D. J., 19
Dreiser, Theodore, 13, 31, 83, 88, 89, 93
Dunsany, Lord, 66, 68, 73, 78, 130n13
Dwight, Timothy, 5
Dyer, Dave (fictional), 34, 44, 100, 112
Dyer, Maud (fictional), 48, 56, 86, 91, 94, 100, 102, 105, 106, 107, 112, 120, 121
Dyer family (fictional), 98, 99

Eddy, Mary Baker, 58
Eden, Martin (fictional), 109
Education, 40, 57, 72, 80–81, 92–93, 109, 123
Egge, Axel (fictional), 48, 50, 52
Eggleston, Edward, 94
Eklund, Oscar (fictional), 95
Elaine (fictional), 27
Elder, Jackson (fictional), 29, 43–44, 68, 69, 71, 95
Eliot, George, 13, 60
Eliot, T. S., 42, 96
Elmer Gantry (Lewis), 6, 9, 42, 109
Elsie Dinsmore books (Finley), 43, 81
Emerson, Ralph Waldo, 12, 32, 88
Erdstrom, Nels (fictional), 60
Erdstrom's son (fictional), 67, 70, 102
Escape, 5, 45, 62, 74–75, 92, 96–97, 109, 112–13, 126–27
Ethan Frome (Wharton), 56
Fables in Slang (Ade), 33

Farrell, James T., 12, 18
Field, Eugene, 94
Fielding, Henry, 17
Fitzgerald, F. Scott, 14, 16, 120
Flanagan, John T., 17
Flandrau, Charles, 42, 72
Flaubert, Gustave, 5, 17, 19
Fleming, Robert E. and Esther, 19
Flickerbaugh, Julius (fictional), 58–59, 72
Flickerbaugh, Mrs. (fictional), 86, 95
Ford, Ford Madox, 15
Ford, Harriet, 15
Forster, E. M., 15
France, Anatole, 93
Frank on the Lower Mississippi (Castlemon), 60
Frank, Waldo, 15
Frederic, Harold, 5, 14, 17, 42, 94, 109
Free Air (Lewis), 4, 38, 43
Freneau, Philip, 5
Freud, Sigmund, 41
Friendship Village (Gale), 5
From Main Street to Stockholm (ed. Smith), 18, 129n4

Gale, Zona, 5, 14, 48, 94
Galsworthy, John, 14
Garland, Hamlin, 4, 5, 15, 19, 94, 111
Gauss, Christian, 17
Geismar, Maxwell, 17
Gibbon, Edward, 81
Gideon Planish (Lewis), 7
Gilbert, Sir William S., 110

The Girl from Kankakee (fictional), 65, 66, 70, 74
Gladstone, William, 69
Glaspell, Susan, 100
The God-Seeker (Lewis), 7
Golden, Una (fictional), 4, 126
Goldfarb, Sam, 130n15
The Good Old Days (Cohn), 30
Gopher Prairie Dramatic Association (fictional), 7, 64, 71
Gopher Prairieites (fictional), 29, 31, 39, 55–56, 70–71, 77, 80, 92, 117
Gould, Dr. Terry (fictional), 68, 92
Gradatim Club, 57
The Grapes of Wrath (Steinbeck), 28
Grebstein, Norman S., 19
"Greenfield Hill" (Dwight), 5
Grote, George, 81
Grundy, Mrs. (fictional), 37
Gurrey, Elisha (fictional), 33

Half a Loaf (Lewis), 18
Hamsun, Knut, 16
Harcourt, Alfred, 8, 13, 14, 18
Harding, Warren G., 6
Hardy, Thomas, 60
Harvard Episodes (Flandrau), 42
Hawthorne, Nathaniel, 32
Haydock, Earl (fictional), 48, 51, 54, 56, 62
Haydock, Harry (fictional), 33, 42, 116
Haydock, Juanita (fictional), 33, 42, 49, 57, 60, 70, 74, 83, 121
Haydock family (fictional), 50, 78, 99, 114, 115, 119, 121
Helmer, Nora (fictional), 126
Hemingway, Ernest, 14
Henty, George A., 81
Hicks, Granville, 17
Hicks, Mrs. (fictional), 52
Hicks, Nat (fictional), 91, 100, 116
High-low motif, 5, 30–31, 37–38, 51, 55, 66, 100, 116–17
The History of Mr. Polly (Wells), 93
Homer, 29
Hoosier Schoolmaster (Eggleston), 94
How He Lied to Her (Shaw), 73
"How I Wrote a Novel on Trains and beside the Kitchen Sink" (Lewis), 129n5
Howe, E. W., 5, 56, 94
Howells, William Dean, 3, 111
Howland, Mrs. (fictional), 55
Hubbard, Elbert, 42
Hume, David, 81
Hunt, Frazer, 16
Hutchinson, Josephine, 17

I Married a Doctor (film), 17, 19
Ibsen, Henrik, 126
The Idea of a University (Newman), 80–81, 130n14
The Idylls of the King (Tennyson), 59
Ingersoll, Ralph, 40
The Innocents (Lewis), 4
"Introduction to *Main Street*" (Lewis), 129n2
"Introduction to *Main Street*" (Van Doren), 17
It Can't Happen Here (Lewis), 7

James, Henry, 26
Jean-Christophe (Rolland), 93
Jennie Gerhardt (Dreiser), 93
Jesus, 41, 82
Joan of Arc, 61
The Job (Lewis), 4, 126
Jolly Seventeen Club (fictional), 47, 48, 49, 50, 52, 53, 54, 55, 56–57, 59, 60, 61, 62, 80, 100, 108
Jones, Howard Mumford, 17

Index

Jorelemon (fictional), 4, 57, 85, 88, 89
Joyce, James, 69

Kafka, Franz, 78
Kazin, Alfred, 17
Keats, John, 60, 103, 108, 110, 111
Keillor, Garrison, 20, 21
Kennicott, Carol (Milford) (fictional), 3–8, 10, 11, 12, 14, 16, 17, 20–22, 25–128; appeal, 36, 70, 89; appearance, 31, 51, 66–67, 78–79, 87, 101, 117; clothes, 32, 51, 67, 78, 87, 101, 117; deceptions, 33, 55, 70, 90–91, 104, 107–8, 121; ego, 37, 54–55, 70, 91, 107, 121; family, 31–32, 50, 66, 79, 102, 104; future, 38, 43, 45–46, 62–63, 65, 75, 83–84, 97, 103, 113, 127–28; house, 37, 39–40, 44, 49, 56, 85, 91–92, 96, 97, 108, 122; imagination, 30, 34, 52–53, 67–68, 78, 87–88, 103–5, 118–19; intellect, 34, 53, 57, 68, 78, 88–89, 91, 102–3, 105; self-knowledge, 36, 53–54, 69, 90, 106, 120–21; self-value, 26, 30–31, 55, 69, 87, 100–101, 116–17; sensations, 35–36, 53, 89–90, 105, 120; sympathies, 33, 51–52, 67, 79–80, 90, 102, 117–18; versatility, 32–33, 74
Kennicott, Hugh (fictional), 76, 79, 80, 81, 82, 83, 84, 86, 88, 90, 95, 97, 102, 104, 105, 107, 114, 115, 117, 118, 123, 126
Kennicott, Mrs. (fictional), 48, 77, 80
Kennicott, Will (fictional), 4, 6, 11, 14, 25, 26, 27, 28, 29, 30, 32, 33, 35, 36, 37, 38, 39, 40, 42, 43, 44, 45, 47, 48, 51, 52, 54, 56, 59, 61–62, 63, 64, 65, 66, 67, 68, 69, 70, 71, 72, 73, 74, 76, 77, 78, 79, 80, 82, 83, 85, 86, 87, 88, 89, 90, 91, 92, 94, 97, 98, 99, 100, 101, 102, 103, 104, 105, 106, 107, 108, 109, 110, 111, 112, 113, 114, 115, 116, 117, 118, 119, 120, 121, 122, 123, 124, 126, 127, 128
Kennicotts' daughter (fictional), 115, 117, 123, 128
Key, Ellen, 93
Kingsblood Royal (Lewis), 7
Kipling, Rudyard, 42, 59
Kirkland, Joseph, 94
Koran, 8

Lac-qui-Meurt (fictional), 48, 53, 54, 62
Lady Chatterley's Lover (Lawrence), 49
Lake Minniemashie (fictional), 49, 51, 53, 62, 83, 89
Lalla Rookh (Moore), 60
Lamb, Charles, 60, 72, 95
The Land of Heart's Desire (Yeats), 73
Larsen, Nella, 20
The Laughter of the Gods (Dunsany), 73, 130n13
Launcelot (fictional), 27
Lawrence, D. H., 49
Lewis at Zenith (ed. Schorer), 19
Lewis, Dorothy Thompson. *See* Thompson, Dorothy
Lewis, Dr. Edwin J., 39
Lewis, Grace Hegger, 5, 18, 32, 37, 94
Lewis, Harry Sinclair, admiration for aviators, explorers, 124; ambivalence toward Sauk Centre, 19, 20, 21, 38; attitude toward intellectuals and artists, 89; birth, 3–4; book reviewer, 41; death, 8; detective stories, 42; early aspira-

tions, 7, 66, 83, 88; early novels, 4, 13, 109; early reading, 60; early travel, 127; faith in progress, 4, 12, 26; Helicon Hall, 43; labor novel, 61; later novels, 7–8; mimicry, 31; need for recognition, 37; Nobel Prize, 7, 18, 61; novels of 1920s, 6; Pulitzer Prize, 6, 15, 19; religion, 40; social/political beliefs, 7, 16, 40, 61, 85; trains, 83; Yale, 121
Lewis, Wells, 79
The Life of Joan of Arc (France), 93
Light, Martin, 19, 20, 24
Literary Renaissance in America (Bechhofer), 16
Literature/drama, 41–43, 58–60, 72–74, 81–82, 93–95, 110–11, 123–24
London, Jack, 109
Longfellow, Henry Wadsworth, 32, 42, 59, 94
Lorimer, George Horace, 58
Love and Marriage (Key), 93
"The Love Song of J. Alfred Prufrock" (Eliot), 96
Lovett, Robert Morss, 15
Ludelmeyer, Frederick F. (fictional), 28, 33
Lundquist, James, 19, 20, 21
Lynd, Robert S. and Helen M., 10, 17

McCarthy, John F., 10, 129n7
McGanum, Dr. (fictional), 68, 92
McGanum, Mrs. (fictional), 55
McPherson, Aimee Semple, 6
Madame Bovary (Flaubert), 5, 19, 106
Madame Butterfly (Puccini), 29
Madden, Celia (fictional), 109
Maggie (Crane), 4
Main Street, play, 15; film, 16
Main Street & Babbitt (Library of America), 21
"Main Street's Been Paved" (Lewis), 16
Main-Travelled Roads (Garland), 4, 94
Major Barbara (Shaw), 93
Malory, Sir Thomas, 129n1
The Man from Main Street (ed. Maule and Cane), 18, 129n2
The Man Who Knew Coolidge (Lewis), 6, 116
Manfred, Frederick, 18, 19
Mankato, Minnesota, 30, 31, 38, 64, 66, 67, 118
Mantrap (Lewis), 6
Marbury family (fictional), 37
Martin Eden (London), 109
Marx, Karl, 61
Masters, Edgar Lee, 5, 93
Maule, Harry E., 18, 129n2
Meeber, Carrie (fictional), 83, 88
Mencken, H. L., 5, 12, 14, 93
Middletown (Lynd and Lynd), 10, 17
Middletown in Transition (Lynd and Lynd), 17
Milford, Hugh (fictional), 7, 32, 50, 67–68, 79, 98, 102, 103
Milton, John, 29, 41, 60
Minneapolis/St. Paul ("the Cities"), 7, 25, 26, 30, 31, 34, 36, 37, 38, 40, 41, 43, 44, 47, 53, 54, 57, 65, 66, 67, 68, 70, 71, 73, 74, 77, 83, 99, 101, 104, 107, 108, 110, 113, 115, 118, 119, 126
Minniemashie House (fictional), 7, 38, 100, 108
Miss Lulu Bett (Gale), 14, 94
Montessori, Maria, 123
Moon-Calf (Dell), 94
Morgenrath, Adolph (fictional), 67
Morse, Ruth (fictional), 109

Index

Morte D'Arthur (Malory), 129n1
Mott, George Edwin (fictional), 29, 35, 40, 48
Mott, Mrs. (fictional), 57, 92
Müller, Max, 41
Mullins, Fern (fictional), 98, 99, 100, 102, 103, 104, 105, 107, 108, 109, 110, 111, 127
The Music Man (Wilson), 122

Narrator, 27–28, 49, 65, 77, 86, 99, 112, 115
Native Son (Wright), 122
Nellie the Beautiful Cloak Model (Davis), 71
Nelson, Lucy (fictional), 19
Newman, John Henry, 80, 130n14
Nexö, Martin Andersen, 93
Nicholson, Meredith, 11, 14, 16, 129n9
Norris, Frank, 34
The Novelist's America (Blake), 19

Oedipus Tyrannus (Sophocles), 74
O. Henry, 42
O'Higgins, Harvey, 15
"An Old Sweetheart of Mine" (Riley), 60
Olson, Roberta, 21
Oscarina (fictional), 80, 85, 92
Othello (Shakespeare), 71
Our Mr. Wrenn (Lewis), 4
Our Town (Wilder), 77

Pamela (Richardson), 5
Parrington, Vernon, 11, 16, 129n8
Pater, Walter, 111
Patience (Gilbert and Sullivan), 110
Pattee, Fred Lewis, 17
Perry, Champ (fictional), 60, 114, 117, 121, 125
Perry, Mrs. (fictional), 52, 55, 57, 114, 117, 125
Perry family (fictional), 49, 50, 53, 55, 58, 61, 70, 79
Petticoat, Warble (fictional), 15
Phelps, William Lyon, 14
Phillips, David Graham, 5
Pioneering, 37, 38, 44, 49, 50, 53, 55, 59, 62, 63, 64
Plot, 14, 26–27, 47–49, 64–65, 76–77, 85–86, 98–99, 114–15
Poe, Edgar Allan, 44
Pollock, Guy (fictional), 34, 35, 36–37, 41, 42, 49, 54, 59, 60, 63, 64, 65, 67, 68, 69, 70, 71–72, 74, 75, 79, 82, 94–95, 96
Poor White (Anderson), 94
Prescott, William Hickling, 81
The Prodigal Parents (Lewis), 7
Ptomaine Street (Wells), 15
"Puritanism as a Literary Force" (Mencken), 93

Quicksand (Larsen), 20
The Quixotic Vision of Sinclair Lewis (Light), 19

Rabelais, François, 41, 94
Rachmaninoff, Sergey, 75
Rankin, Hugh, 79
Realism, 4, 6, 10, 11, 12, 13, 14, 38, 39, 67, 69, 82, 99, 127, 128
"The Recessional" (Kipling), 60
Religion, 36, 40–41, 58, 71–72, 82–83, 92, 108, 110, 123
Repplier, Agnes, 42
"The Revolt from the Village: 1920" (Van Doren), 15
The Revolt from the Village: 1915–1930 (Hilfer), 19
The Revolt of the Angels (France), 93
Richardson, Samuel, 5
Riley, James Whitcomb, 14, 59

The Rise of Silas Lapham (Howells), 3
Rocky Mountains, 26, 31, 35, 45, 49, 51, 62, 78, 87, 88, 120
Rolland, Romain, 41, 93
Romanticism, 4, 10, 11, 12, 19, 21, 30, 38, 64, 67, 69, 71, 88, 95, 118, 119, 123, 127
Romeo and Juliet (Shakespeare), 74
Roosevelt, Theodore, 5
"A Rose for Little Eva" (Lewis), 38
Rose of Dutcher's Coolly (Garland), 5
Rossetti, Dante Gabriel, 60
Roth, Philip, 12, 19
Rustad, Helga (fictional), 33
Rustad, Pete (fictional), 30, 33, 34, 39, 51

Sappho, 27
Satire, 11, 13, 14, 21, 28–29, 40, 49–50, 65, 77–78, 99–100, 116
Sauk Centre, Minnesota, 3, 8, 10, 12, 14, 17, 18, 19, 20, 21, 31, 39, 59, 60, 71
The Scarlet Letter (Hawthorne), 104
Schmaltz, Lowell T. (fictional), 116
Schnitzler, Arthur, 73
The School for Scandal (Sheridan), 74
Schoenstrom (fictional), 4–5, 43, 46
Schorer, Mark, 9, 18–19, 28, 31, 129n3
Scott, Sir Walter, 60
Sentimentality, 4, 37, 65, 96, 111, 116, 125
Shakespeare, William, 60
Shaw, George Bernard, 5, 41, 65, 73, 74, 93, 111
Shelley, Percy Bysshe, 110
Sherman, Stuart Pratt, 15
Sherwin, Vida. *See* Wutherspoon, Vida
"Significance of the Frontier in American History" (Turner), 4
Simon, Rita (fictional), 54
Sinclair Lewis (Lundquist), 19, 20
Sinclair Lewis: A Reference Guide (Fleming and Fleming), 19
Sinclair Lewis: An American Life (Schorer), 18, 129n6
Sinclair Lewis at 100 (ed. Connaughton), 20
The Sinclair Lewis Newsletter, 19
The Sinclair Lewis Society, 21
Sinclair Lewis: The Journey (Olson), 20
Sinclair, Upton, 43
Sister Carrie (Dreiser), 93
Smail, Bessie (fictional), 76, 78, 80, 82, 88, 103, 108
Smail, Whittier N. (fictional), 76, 78, 80, 81, 87, 103
Smail family (fictional), 77–78, 80, 81, 82
Smith, Harrison, 18, 129n4
Snaffin, Del (fictional), 116
Snyder, Stewart (fictional), 27, 36, 45
Social/political issues, 43–44, 61, 72, 81, 91, 92, 95, 108–9, 124–25
"The Song of Hiawatha" (Longfellow), 59
Sorenson, Bea. *See* Bjornstam, Bea
Spencer, Theodore, 129n1
Spindler, Michael, 19–20
Spoon River Anthology (Masters), 93, 94
Steele, Wilbur Daniel, 16
Steinbeck, John, 28
Stevenson, Robert Louis, 60
The Story of a Country Town (Howe), 56, 94
Stowbody, Ella (fictional), 43, 95
Stowbody, Ezra (fictional), 43, 95
Straws and Prayer Books (Cabell), 16

Stribling, T. S., 20
Strindberg, August, 87, 94
Structure, 5, 10–11, 22, 25
Style, 5, 11, 14, 19, 21
Sullivan, Sir Arthur, 110
Sunday, Billy, 6
Suppressed Desires (Glaspell), 100
Susan Lenox (Phillips), 5
Swede Hollow (fictional), 61, 62
Swiftwaite, Mrs. (fictional), 98, 101, 107
Swinburne, A. C., 60
Sycamore Bend (Hunt), 16
Symbolism, 11, 12, 30, 31, 35, 37–38, 51, 55, 66, 79, 83, 100, 101, 104, 108, 116–17
Symons, Arthur, 42

Taft, William Howard, 5
Tarkington, Booth, 14
The Tattooed Countess (Van Vechten), 16
Tennyson, Alfred, Lord, 27, 59, 60
Tess of the D'Urbervilles (Hardy), 5
Thackeray, W. M., 60
Thanatopsis Club, 7, 35, 48, 49, 50, 52, 53, 54, 55, 57, 58, 60, 61, 62
Thompson, Dorothy, 18
Thoreau, Henry David, 12, 32, 41, 42
Time, 10, 26, 35
Tolstoy, Leo, 5, 60, 61
Tono-Bungay (Wells), 93
The Trail of the Hawk (Lewis), 4
Trains, 28, 29, 31, 34, 68, 76, 82, 83, 88, 114, 118
Turner, Frederick Jackson, 3–4
Twain, Mark, 3, 5, 29
The Two Orphans (D'Ennery), 71

Ulysses (Joyce), 69
Updike, John, 12
Upson, Arthur, 110

Valborg, Adolph (fictional), 99, 101, 108, 109, 110, 111, 112, 113
Valborg, Erik (fictional), 7, 26, 98, 99, 100, 101, 102, 103, 104, 105, 106, 107, 108, 109, 110, 112, 113, 114, 115, 118, 119, 124, 126, 127
The Valley of Democracy (Nicholson), 14
Van Doren, Carl, 15, 17
Van Vechten, Carl, 16
Veblen, Thorstein, 5, 60, 88, 93
Vidor, Florence, 16
Villets, Ethel (fictional), 55, 59
Voltaire, 5, 40

Wakamin (fictional), 57, 59, 85, 125
Walden (Thoreau), 36
Walpole, Hugh, 79
Ward, Mrs. Humphrey, 60
Ware, Theron (fictional), 109
Warner, Isabel, 57
Warren, Mrs. (fictional), 48, 58
Washburn, Claude, 42
Washington, D.C., 6, 26, 115, 116, 117, 118, 120, 121, 122, 123, 124, 125, 126, 127
Washington, Martha, 29
Wells, Carolyn, 15
Wells, H. G., 79, 93, 128
West, Rebecca, 15
Westlake, Dr. (fictional), 68, 72, 81, 116
Westlake, Mrs. (fictional), 60, 61, 85, 86, 91, 97
Wharton, Edith, 5, 14, 15, 16, 56
When She Was Good (Roth), 19
White, William Allen, 14, 16
Whittier, John Greenleaf, 29
Wilder, Thorton, 77
Wilks, Mary Ellen (fictional), 58
Willard, George (fictional), 83
Wilson, Meredith, 122

Wilson, Woodrow, 3, 5, 8
Windy McPherson's Son (Anderson), 94
Winesburg, Ohio (Anderson), 82, 93–94
With Love from Gracie (Lewis), 18
Wolfe, Thomas, 78
The Woman Movement (Key), 93
Wood, Grant, 20
Woolf, Virginia, 15
Work of Art (Lewis), 7
World So Wide (Lewis), 8
World War I, 4, 5, 12, 76, 85, 92, 95, 114, 125–26
Wright, Harold Bell, 60
Wright, Richard, 12, 122
Wutherspoon, Raymond (fictional), 27, 29, 33, 36, 42–43, 74, 77, 78, 81, 82, 86, 90, 92, 93, 125–26
Wutherspoon, Vida (fictional), 28, 35, 40, 41, 42, 46, 47, 49, 51, 54, 55, 57, 61, 62, 72, 74, 76, 77, 78, 81, 82, 85, 86, 87, 88, 89, 90, 91, 92, 93, 94, 969, 99, 102, 106, 108, 114, 121, 123, 124, 125, 127

Yeats, W. B., 52, 59, 68, 73, 129n12

Zenobia, 27
Zitterel, Mrs. (fictional), 94
Zitterel, the Reverend Edmund (fictional), 82, 99, 105, 108, 110, 111, 124
Zury (Kirkland), 94

The Author

Martin Bucco is a professor of English at Colorado State University. He is the author of numerous books, among them *The Voluntary Tongue* (1957), *Frank Waters* (1969), *Wilbur Daniel Steele* (1972), *E. W. Howe* (1977), *René Wellek* (1981), and *Western American Literary Criticism* (1984), and the editor of *Critical Essays on Sinclair Lewis* (1986). He has also written many scholarly reviews and essays on American authors and their writings. The recipient of several grants from the National Endowment for the Humanities and a John N. Stern Distinguished Professor Award from Colorado State, he has served as president and executive secretary of the Western Literature Association and is on the editorial boards of *Western American Literature* and *Rocky Mountain Review.*

	DATE DUE		

North Haven High School
LIBRARY MEDIA CENTER
North Haven, CT